MY LOST CHILDHOOD

A Prussian Family

Under the Hitler Regime

By

Marli Wedgeworth

Copyright © 2025 by Marli Wedgeworth

All rights reserved. No part of this book may be reproduced or transmitted in any form or by any means without written permission from the author.

Table of Contents

Foreword ii
About the Author iv
Introduction 2
    The Powerlessness of the Weimar Republic after World War I 2
    The Rise of the NSDAP 3
    The Magnetism of the Nazis 3
    Hitler is Appointed Chancellor 4
    Nationalistic Government: The Nazis Divide the Power 4
    Reichstagsbrand: First Step toward Dictatorship 5
    Oppression of Adversaries 6
    Hitler Gains More Power 6
    Alignment of Society 7
    Oppression of Jews 7
Introduction of Main Characters 9
World War I: July 1914 - November 1918 21
January 30, 1933 – Hitler was appointed Chancellor, and Germany became a Dictatorship 27
Berlin 1937 31
November 9, 1938 48
1939 49
    (1933-1939) Divided into Three Periods: 51
    Anti-Jewish Policy by Year 51

1939 – 1940 Poland 56

1942 61

April 19, 1943 73

1945 74

April until July 1945 - American Occupation of Thuringia
.... 83

July 2, 1945 – Arrival of the Russians 85

Berlin Blockade 1948/1949 – Die Rosinenbomber – The C-47 Candy Bombers 88

Back in Thuringia 96

1948 – A New Beginning 104

1951 108

Fall of 1956 129

This book is dedicated to my family and in deep devotion to my late love, Jerome W. Keyes, Jr.

Foreword

Before I decided to write this book, I did not realize that war would break out between the Hamas and the Israelis. This is most unfortunate. I do not intend to hurt anyone's feelings, but my book and its content have been on my mind for years, ever since I realized how much injustice exists in this world.

My book was written to remind humanity how wars bring destruction, grief, pain, and sorrow. Wars not only destroy buildings and artifacts of great value from past centuries, which mean so much to the people who live there and to others, but they kill lives and cause upheaval and confusion.

We all believe in ONE God! Just because we have different denominations does not mean we should hate one another. My book not only tells my tale of how I grew up, but it touches on the fate of our Jewish brothers and sisters as well, who suffered throughout the centuries.

People do not realize how they were being persecuted, chased, and tortured – whenever people wanted to blame someone. They used them as their scapegoat. People, who have not studied history do not know the truth. I could write books about the miseries and pains Jewish people had to suffer – human beings just like you and I, who were envied, and degraded.

Students, who do not know the truth about the Jewish fate, are protesting now in colleges. Muslims condemn Jewish people, who have no choice but to defend themselves. The Arab world would love to see them drown in the sea and wipe them off this earth. Where is "love your neighbor like you love yourself?" The Jewish population occupied their land with the Arabs centuries ago.

The Jewish occupants have to fight for themselves because evil has been sewn upon them. I have followed their history. Their plight has moved my heart and my senses. Therefore, I wrote this book to make people realize that force and violence are not the answer to problems. Every time the population expands, there is greed to gain land and wars always start in the name of religion.

I suffered dearly during my childhood and so did millions along with me. I do not wish it onto anyone – think of the children. Who wants to be born into a world of hostility and wars?

About the Author

Marli Wedgeworth, who was born in Germany, embarked on an educational path that carried her through a private high school to the revered halls of Cambridge University in London, England. At the scenic Vorbeck School for Foreign Correspondents in Germany's Black Forest, she further refined her skills. She traveled over the Atlantic to enroll in college in the United States.

With a passion for language, she contributed to the learning landscape by teaching English in Adult Education in Bavaria, Germany. Marli's career path brought her to engage with American businesses, promoting intercultural understanding while she was employed in Germany and the US. The author's storytelling is surely enhanced by her diversified background and global viewpoint, which provide readers with an insight into a world influenced by a multitude of experiences and cultural intersections.

"Injustice is the greatest evil of humanity."

-Socrates, a man of principle

Introduction

*GERMANY 1933: FROM DEMOCRACY TO DICTATORSHIP

1933, Hitler gains power and changes Germany from a Republic into a Dictatorship.

The Powerlessness of the Weimar Republic after World War I

Germany has been a Republic since 1919. After the defeat of World War I, Emperor Wilhelm II abdicated. Most Germans are not satisfied with the new situation. They want their Emperor back. Besides, many Bürger believe that the governing Social Democrats are guilty of Germany's defeat. Although in the middle of the 20th- century, things are improving.

1930, it is the end. Because of worldwide depression, Germany is not capable of paying the war debts, which were set in the Versailles Peace Contract.

Millions of Germans lose their jobs. Also, politics enter a crisis. Cabinets plunge and constantly lead to new elections. It seems impossible to form a majority government.

The Rise of the NSDAP

Behind these scenes, the rise of the National German Workers Party (NSDAP) occurs. 1920, her organization is a small party. Hitler, with his talkative talents, manages to accumulate more members. Its extreme Nationalism and Antisemitism mark the party.

November 1923 - Hitler tries, through a putsch, to seize power. With it, he completely fails. Hitler ends up behind bars, and the judge forbids the NSDAP. At the end of 1924, after a rather small fine, Hitler is set free. His political career is not finished. In prison, he writes "Mein Kampf" (My Struggle) and displays his plans for Germany.

Henceforth, the Nazis follow the legal way and try to win power through an election. They profit from the depression, which started in the twenties. They use this crisis through profuse criticism against the government and the Versailles Contract.

Their strategy works. In 1928, the NSDAP receives 0,8 election votes; in 1930, the election numbers rises to 6,4 million.

The Magnetism of the Nazis

The reason that so many Germans feel drawn to the NSDAP has nothing to do with the party program. The party radiates strength and dynamics. Besides, the Nazi leaders are young, different from the grey-headed politicians of the established parties, and Hitler's image of a strong leader kindles fantasies. Many see in him who can unite the people and end political disputes.

The Nazis turn to female voters and male voters from every social class, not just to single groups like blue-collared workers or Catholics. They reach many people, including people who do not vote. Despite this, it looks like they reached their height in 1932. Once more, the economy gets going, and the NSDAP loses 15% of its seats, even though it remains the strongest of all parties.

Hitler is Appointed Chancellor

The conservative parties do not receive enough support from the population. They pressure Chancellor Paul von Hindenburg to appoint Hitler as Chancellor. They hope, together with the NSDAP, to form a majority government. Their expectation that Hitler would include their agenda will prove to be a fatal misjudgment.

January 30, 1933 – the time comes that Hindenburg relents and appoints Hitler as Chancellor. "It is almost a dream. The Wilhemstraße (place of Parliament) is ours", writes Propaganda minister Joseph Goebbels in his diary. Hitler is elected by the people and, therefore, gains power the legal way.

Nationalistic Government: The Nazis Divide the Power

The Nationalists celebrate their victory with a torchlight procession through Berlin. Hitler watches approvingly from the balcony of the Reich Chancellory. He is anything but omnipotent currently. The NSDAP must work together with other parties of the right spectrum.

In the new government, only two NSDAP party members are present - Wilhelm Frick and Hermann Göring. Hitler ensures that they take important positions.

Of great importance is the role that Hermann Göring plays. He is a Minister without a business and receives control over the police of Prussia, the biggest part of Germany. For the Nazis, it is reason enough to celebrate the "national revolution," but many Germans take in this news by shrugging their shoulders. They have seen governments come and go and expect that the new government will not last very long.

Reichstagsbrand: First Step toward Dictatorship
Shortly after, Hitler seizes more power. A key event is the fire of the Government building. February 27, 1933, the watchmen discover that the building stands in flame. They overwhelm the suspected arsonist, a Dutch communist by the name of Marinus von der Lubbe. He will be executed by a show trial. If he has accomplices, it will never be clarified.

The Nazi leaders are on the spot quickly. The latter Gestapo chief Rudolf Diels is present and reports, Göring: "This is the beginning of the communistic revolt; they will strike now! Not a minute has to be wasted!" Before he could continue, Hitler roars: "There is no mercy now; whoever gets in our way gets put down."

Chancellor Hindenburg proclaims the next day the "Decree of the Chancellor for the Protection of the People and State," also called The Reichstag Fire Decree. That creates the basis for dictatorship.

The civil rights of the population are restricted. Freedom of speech is no longer a matter of course, and the police can arbitrarily search houses and arrest people. Political opponents of the Nazis now become outlaws.

Oppression of Adversaries
In this atmosphere of intimidation on March 5, 1933, new elections take place. In the streetscape, posters and NSDAP flags dominate. Despite this, the hope for great victory does not materialize. With 43. 9 percent, the NSDAP does not reach the majority. The left parties KPF and SPD, still achieve 30% votes.

The arrests and intimidation increase. The government forbids the Communist Party. On March 15, ten thousand communists are arrested. To accommodate all of the political prisoners, the first concentration camps are opened. The circumstances in these are dreadful. Prisoners are beaten and tortured, and some are murdered.

Especially Jewish people and well-known individuals are having a difficult time. So, lead SS guards in the Dachau camp near Munich took four Jewish prisoners and shot them in front of the camp gate. The guards claim the victims tried to flee.

Hitler Gains More Power
March 23, 1933 – Parliament in Berlin is in session. A new law is on the agenda, "The Enabling Act (Ermächtigungsgesetz)." It enables Hitler to legislate laws for four years without the interference of the Chancellor, the Counsel, and the Parliament. The parliament building is surrounded by men of

the SA and the SS, paramilitary organizations of the NSDAP, called Auxiliary Police.

Hitler affronts the delegates with his decision, "War or Peace."

That is a hidden warning to intimidate persons who want to vote against it. There is no sign of talk of a democratic vote. With 444 votes with 'yes' and 94 dissenting votes, Parliament accepts the Enabling Act. Until 1945, it has become the fundamentals of the Nazi dictatorship.

Alignment of Society

After Hitler amasses too much power, the Nazis begin to change society after their images. This process is called alignment. Jewish and politically unpopular civil servants are discharged. Trade Unions are terminated; instead, they create the German Work Front. This way, the Nazis prevent workers to organize themselves against the government.

The existing political parties are forbidden. As of the middle of July 1933, Germany is a one-party state. Also, in cultural and scientific fields, "purges" (Säuberungen) take place. Everything 'Un-German' is to disappear. The Nazis burn books, above all Jewish, left, and pacified writers.

Oppression of Jews

In the phase of seizure of power, Nazi destruction is mainly aimed at political opponents. An exception is, Jewish citizens of Germany. As a group, they do not form an opposition against Nazi politics. Regardless, they become victims of violence, harassment, and oppression. In April 1933, the regime takes official action against Jewish Germans. They announced a nationwide Boycott against Jewish stores. It is the first step, among a row of other anti-Jewish measures, which will end with the Holocaust.

Hitler is the sole ruler. Hitler and the Nazis, after their takeover, turn Germany into a dictatorship. They always turn to legal means to maintain the appearance of legality. Step by step, Hitler underminds democracy, until it's just a façade. However, the process does not end there. In the twelve years the Third Reich existed, Hitler continues to consolidate his rule.

Translated from German into English.

* www.annefrank.org

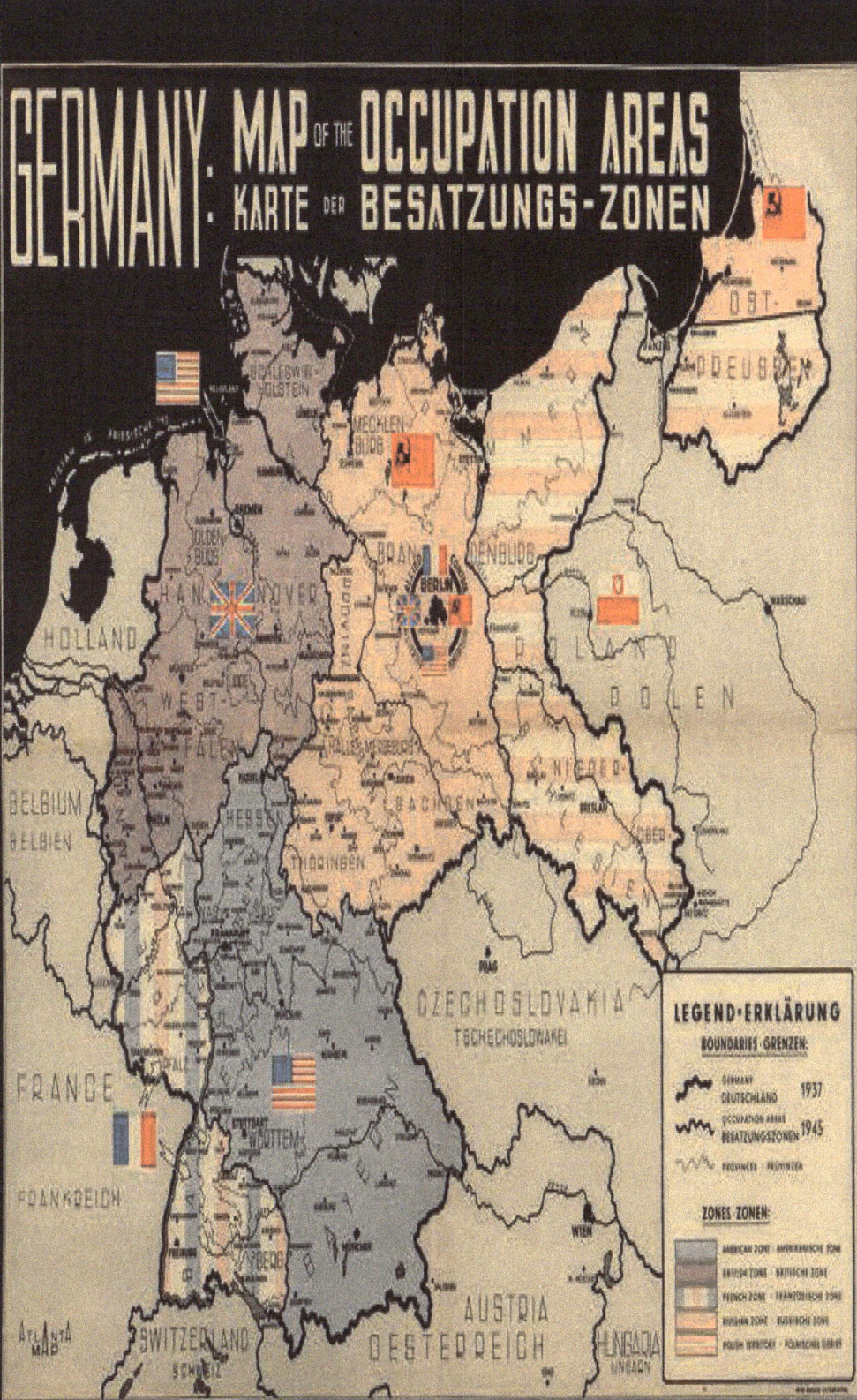

Introduction of Main Characters

- My father: Dr.-jur. Horst H. Ganske, Attorney at Law
- My mother: Annaliese, born Herford
- My grandfather: Dr. Franz Ganske
- My grandmother: Margot Ganske, maiden name: Kanter
- Two sons: Horst Herman Ganske, and Franz Ganske
- Diplom-Engineer Franz Ganske and his wife Erika
- Three sons: Nickolaus, Thomas, and Michael
- My grandmother Margot's three siblings:
- Dr. (med.) Ernst Kanter, eye doctor, and his wife Käthe
- Elizabeth (Liesel) Kanter, her husband, Professor Dr. Phil. Barth,
- Dr. med. Hermann Kanter, his wife Rosel

Numerous friends and relatives will appear throughout my book.

My story covers several generations, who, by the end of World War II, would be scattered and displaced all over Germany, which ended in such a pathetic manner - a typical bourgeoisie family, who at one time owned large properties. In our families, we had pastors, medical doctors, teachers, lawyers, tradesmen, blacksmiths, and large landowners. On my grandmother's side, some centuries ago, they immigrated from Salzburg, Austria, and relocated to Silesia (Schlesien), Germany. My grandfather's side originated from Bohemia and later relocated to Prussia.

(After World War II, Silesia and Bohemia were annexed by the Polish/Czech Republic). According to my grandmother, we were a close-knit family, frequently visiting back and forth. Most families lived on land parcels side by side. Some of them resettled in Prussia due to religious wars between the Catholics and the Protestants. Our families decided to choose the Protestant religion.

My grandmother Margot, grandfather Dr. Franz Ganske; brother Dr. Ernst Kanter (eye-doc), wife Käthe; sister Liesel, husband Prof Dr. Phil Barth; brother Dr. med. Hermann Kanter, wife Rosel

Father of my grandmother, Dr. Herman Kanter

Grandma as a young woman

My grandfather married to my grandmother, Dr. Franz Ganske

My grandmother Margot with my Dad Horst and my Uncle Franz

To this day, wars are raging throughout the world, causing destruction and starvation. Children grow up surrounded by terror and continuous nightmares, which will forever be imprinted in their minds. I was one of these unfortunate children, which caused deep wounds and distress in my life, but made me a better person who learned to understand other people's pains.

I was modeled after the images of my ancestors, who were well-educated and hard-working folks with high moral standards. I was taught to respect values, be polite, and be tolerant toward others. While adults would have conversations with each other, children were not to interrupt them and were only allowed to speak when spoken to. Education was highly valued and appreciated. Correct table mannerism was taught at an early age - how to use cutlery at the table, sit straight in a chair, and stand behind a chair until the hostess sat down. We called our parents' friends "Aunts and Uncles." Girls curtsied, and boys clicked their heels. We shook hands with one another.

 My father wanted me to follow in his profession as a lawyer, which would not have suited me because I preferred the humanistic way showing a great love for books, history, arts, and nature. It also was a time when women were groomed to get married (unter die Haube kommen, get under the bonnet). After the Second World War, this idiotic arrangement finally changed and so did our strict class system. My grandmother had the privilege to visit the Conservatory of Music, which would be to her advantage. She raised her two sons by teaching piano to upgrade her widow's pension after her husband passed away at the early age of 60 years.

My Dad and my Uncle Franz, very fashionable in sailor suits

Vigorous conversations around meal tables were appreciated and inspiring. My father's immense knowledge of history and government matters and surrounding himself with interesting friends made a lasting impression on me. In my grandfather's humanistic high school, my father learned Latin, Greek, and French, with one year of English.

After my grandfather's early death, my grandmother lived in a generously laid out flat with her younger son Franz in Steglitz, Berlin.

Here are excerpts from her memoirs during World War II:

"On March 1942, my first firebomb burned out one room in my flat on Kissinger Street. This was a first warning, which forced me to send some of my belongings to Altenburg in Thüringen (Thuringia), where my two brothers live with their families. On January 29, 1943, my son's beautiful flat in Wilmersdorf, Berlin, burned out caused by firebombs. That afternoon I was by myself. With the help of waggoneers and their horses, since my son's furniture was standing in the street, it, at last, was brought to my flat. On January 30, I was not able to make it to the air raid cellar in time. Hell broke loose around me and the world seemed to crash down upon us. Throughout the night, all of Berlin burned. During the night I managed to stand on the skeleton of a roof, trying to extinguish the sparks. At four o'clock in the morning, we were ordered to evacuate our houses, since two unexploded bombs could detonate any minute and destroy all of us. On foot, I managed to reach Mica's apartment (relative) on Meineke Street. My final sanctuary was Altenburg in Thüringen (Thuringia), with endless trips between Berlin and my destination, to get the rest of the furniture per ship to Landsberg a.d. Warthe, since transport wagons are no longer available.

Everything is lost – including our dignity. Poor Germany! May our grandchildren find a way out of this hell."

My grandmother taught me to be resilient and face life with courage. Her wisdom and courage helped me to become the person I am today. The most important things are, never giving up on accumulating knowledge and education, appreciating arts, enjoying beautiful music and opera, and respecting nature with its magnificent animals. My grandmother, together with my family, had to live and suffer through two wars - World War I and World War II.

World War I: July 1914 - November 1918

It is one of the deadliest global conflicts in history. Millions died. Germany lost the war, and a treaty was signed in the Palace of Versailles, France, on June 28, 1919, forcing Germany to pay enormous sums of reparation for damages done. The German Emperor abdicated and was accepted by the Dutch government to live the rest of his life in Holland. Inflation reached its height in 1923. Grandmother told me, *"We ground acorn and chestnuts as a coffee substitute, together with other mixtures, in Grandpa's Turkish coffee grinder* (which I still possess). *We were hungry. Money was worthless, even though the government kept printing money. One loaf of bread would cost millions of marks, and the next day it reached billions. People were asked to use their wages immediately and purchase what foods were available. Unemployment raged and inflation exploded."*

Later, this would be the breeding ground for the Nazis. I still can hear her loud and scolding voice exclaiming in utter distaste and dislike *"That man Hitler will lead all of us to hell and destroy our beautiful country."* How often would we have to be reminded of her warning words at family gatherings? My Dad would tell her to be quiet. His words: *"You will bring all of us into a concentration camp, or we will be shot."* People seemed to be totally mesmerized by the Nazis, or simply too afraid to speak up. People claimed he brought order and put butter back on their tables. Among his fanatic followers were my uncle's wife, Aunt Erika, and my stepmother Uschi. Both adored Hitler and cried bitterly when he committed suicide.

Turkish Coffee Grinder brought back by my grandfather, used during World War I

My grandmother played a big role in my life since I had been abandoned by my mother and had no siblings. Dad and grandmother were the two most important people. She may have been strict and old-fashioned at times, worried that I would carry my mother's genes in me and could follow in her footsteps - with my mother's endless marriages.

She might have been overly cautious, but she still took care of me in times of adversity. Besides teaching me to play the piano, a love for arts, good books, opera, and classical music, I also learned how to sew on her old Singer treadle sewing machine, embroider, knit, and crochet. Both my father and my grandmother taught me to be tolerant towards other people and not be judgmental.

After reading my grandmother's diary about our family and about my grandfather's ancestry, I learned that in the 18th century, her family migrated from Salzburg, Austria to Silesia (Schlesien), after a disastrous pestilence raged throughout Europe during the 30-Year War. We are related to the renowned painter Willy Höhnel of Austria, of whom I have a small painting. Dad would often tell me there was a great resemblance between me and my cousins in Austria. My grandmother was a Kanter, which is a Jewish name. She denied this vehemently in her memoirs, probably because under Hitler non-Ariens were not tolerated. She insisted that the Kanters came from Salzburg, Austria, and were farmers and not related to our Jewish ancestors, which she claimed were a sideline of the Kanters. What difference would that make?

On my father's side, they came from Bohemia and settled in Prussia.

We were 'von Ganzky' and possessed a beautiful large Crest. My grandfather dropped the 'von' and it simply became 'Ganske.' My grandmother wrote that Grandpa would talk very lovingly about his Polish grandmother as being a highly intelligent and witty lady. My grandmother met my grandfather, Dr. Franz Ganske, in Marienburg in Prussia, where he fell in love with her, but he did not dare propose to her until later. My grandmother told me, my grandfather was a wonderful, kind, and very educated man. He would simply have adored me since there were only boys in our immediate family.

After my grandfather returned to Prussia from Constantinople (Turkey), now Istanbul, he was offered and accepted the position of Headmaster at the Humanistic Hufengymnasium in Königsberg, Prussia. He spent years as a Professor at the University of Constantinople and spoke five languages. After he married my grandmother, they had two boys: my dad Horst, and my uncle Franz. As it was customary in those days, both boys had several first names. In my grandfather's school, the students were taught Latin, Greek, French, and English.

After World War II, any graduates alive from his school would mostly settle with their families around Munich, in the State of Bavaria, Germany. They all knew each other and there was an undeniable bond between these friends. The famous German poet Ernst Wiechert had been a teacher in Grandpa's school.

I consider myself a liberal, kind, caring individual, and eager to improve my learning. Having been brought up during violent times and often suffering through other people's cruelty, made me a more understanding person toward indigenous peoples. Freedom and freedom of speech are the two most important things in life, nurtured and cared for like a precious jewel. In 1956, I found it in this country, after I first set foot on American soil. I also appreciate Socrates' philosophy.

Born in Germany in 1934 before World War II, as a little girl looking back, I treasured the few days and years of normalcy in Berlin before the war broke out in Poland in 1939. Hitler needed Lebensraum (living space) and had long decided to annex Silesia into Germany, together with all countries where German citizens had settled for centuries. Hitler told Prime Minister Neville Chamberlain of England (from 1937 to 1940) that he would not take over Czechoslovakia. Chamberlain returned to England telling his people that "all is well," which has gone down in history as 'appeasement.' Next, Hitler invaded Poland and annexed the German-speaking parts into the Reich.

My family was large with many relatives. Our family members would be scattered all about after the war and what was left of Germany. My dad Horst and his brother Franz were born in Deutsch Eylau; my dad in 1905, and Franz in 1906. After their father accepted the position of Headmaster in Königsberg, Dad and my Uncle Franz spent a wonderful childhood there.

Among one of his friends was his everlasting friendship with Uncle Harry von Rosen, together with another friend. Uncle Harry writes in his memoirs, *"We became an inseparable trio."* My grandfather, Dr. Franz Ganske, taught them Latin in his class and Uncle Harry remembered in his memoirs, *"He taught us Roman poetry and I remember the verse 'Da mi basia mille, bis basia mille', give me 1000 kisses and again 1000 kisses. Dr. Ganske also offered to help us to draft love letters."*

Uncle Franz became an engineer and flew airplanes. At the same time, my father pursued his studies in Jurisprudence, majoring in law and political science in the cities of Munich in Bavaria, Vienna in Austria, Breslau in Silesia, and Königsberg (Kaliningrad) in West Prussia. He later served on various courts of law. After he graduated from the University in Königsberg on May 21, 1930, he passed his doctoral exam 'cum laude.' On January 16, 1932, his published dissertation was 'Processes of Fraud and Adequacy.' After Dad passed his Assessor Exam, he was appointed as a judge. Following that, he worked for the Bank of Industry as an Association Manager and Attorney. Later, he opened his practice above the famous Café Kranzler in Berlin, one of the best-remembered cafes in Berlin, which recently closed forever.

I found an article in one of my photo albums, in which I read that my Dad was in *"Who's Who in Germany"*.

Uncle Franz and his wife Erika settled with their three sons in Charlottenburg, Berlin. Her parents had lived many years in China. My aunt had a wonderful mother, who later in life, would play a very important role in their daily lives.

We also frequently visited my Aunt Liesel, my grandmother's sister, in Prussia. She had a housekeeper, whom she called a "Pearl" and who was an essential part of their family. Her children, being my cousins, were of importance to me. I adored her eighteen-year-old son because of his looks and his height, but he would be summoned into the war against Russia and die on the front, barely eighteen years of age. I was inconsolable. I had met the family before the beginning of World War II.

January 30, 1933 – Hitler was appointed Chancellor, and Germany became a Dictatorship

My Dad enjoyed the vibrant life in Berlin. He made friends with famous artists of the theatre, arts, and writers. One of his best friends was Erich Kästner, the famous writer of children's books, and Comedian Werner Fink, whose friendship endured a lifetime. During the Hitler time, Uncle Werner Fink was thrown into a concentration camp because of his untimely remarks made about Hitler in his cabaret '*Die Wühlmäuse.*'

My father bailed him out.

Heinz Sielman was a good friend, who not only was a brilliant photographer and author of many well-known books, but also an animal lover and protector. Heinz Sielman lost his only son under tragic circumstances in Nairobi, Africa. Rudi Platte, a famous stage actor and singer, and many others. (I saw Rudi on stage with my husband in Berlin, at a performance of "My Fair Lady", which was done to perfection). My Dad told me, they saw Marlene Dietrich off on her way on a train and plane to the U.S.A.

Shortly, before a holiday in 1933, my father called his friend Uncle Harry to say that he had the intention to visit his 'aunt' (a cousin, who was related to us through marriage to my grandmother's father, after his wife died). She lived in Forst a. d. Neiße near Breslau, Silesia. They knew she had married a wealthy textile manufacturer, twenty years her Senior. Her husband was of stocky build and medium height. My father told me he found an enchanting young creature, twenty-eight years of age, slender and charming. She had dark hair and blue eyes. Her name was Annaliese, Li for short.

My father instantly fell in love. She confided in him how bitterly disappointed and bored she was in her marriage. Her parents married her off when she was at the young age of eighteen. I later harbored the suspicion that she was pregnant by a lover before her first marriage to such a much older man. She would continue meeting her lover in a resort at the Baltic Sea, a professor, whose distinctive nose was inherited by her first son. Her sister, my Aunt Tü, told me this story much later after I was a grown woman. She had to lie about her sister taking vacations from time to time, even though my mother was married.

My mother had two sons, was endowed with beautiful jewelry, was one of the first ladies who owned a car, had a chauffeur, a nanny, a cook, a gardener, and other personnel. They lived in a beautiful mansion on large grounds, among an extensive family on her husband's side. After she left her first husband, I was told later by one of her sons, who were, when she left, ten and twelve years old, how much they missed their mother. Later in life, I saw a photo of this large family taken in their mansion.

After Dad and Uncle Harry von Rosen arrived at her beautiful grounds, her chauffeur drove Uncle Harry and her boys to the river Neiße where they went swimming. My father stayed with his 'aunt' and faced the battle to free her from her marriage after her husband returned to their villa. My father made the mistake of telling his friend Harry, *"I had to free her from her marriage yoke; otherwise, she would have committed suicide."*

It came to a terrible quarrel between my father, her husband, and her. At last, her husband declared he would release her, but without her attaining custody of her two sons. Hastily, her items were gathered and stowed in Dad's car. The three continued their travel, and his friend Harry left them in Dresden to visit his grandfather. Dad and Li (Annaliese), as she was called for short, moved in with my grandmother and Uncle Franz in Berlin. Because of a criminal charge made by my mother's deserted husband, Dad lost his job. He soon found another position and settled into an office above the Café Kranzler in Berlin. Of course, my mother got pregnant right away. I was born on June 9, 1934. My father had done well financially and was able to purchase a lovely little house in the suburbia of Kleinmachnow. Since he traveled extensively, he took his wife with him and left his little daughter in the care of a housekeeper.

Now to my mother. She was born into a family with three other siblings. Her father was a medical doctor. They were a distinguished family. Their ancestry dates back to Prussia with mostly ranchers. Her sister, my Aunt Tü (I do not have another name for her), was my favorite. She was a highly educated woman with a Master's degree and taught as a college professor. She was of slender build and capricious, full of historical stories, and married twice in two good marriages. After losing her second husband she developed asthma and was very unhappy to be alone. She told me that she danced on top of a table at a party and rode her Vespa with her husband in the backseat. A third sister married and lived in Austria. Her only brother became a minister. Their mother was a rather rotund lady and idolized my mother. I don't remember my grandparents on my mother's side.

I remember our first house in Kleinmachnow with the garden and spending time pulling out the strawberry plants after my father planted them. I remember sitting on the potty surrounded by a tray with toys, bored and, for what seemed like an endless time, only being in the care of the housekeeper. One time, I slid down the stairs in that three-story house into the basement where I caught pneumonia.

Berlin 1937

Since my mother did not like the suburbs and longed for the glitzy Berlin nightlife, my father sold our little house where I was born and purchased a beautiful roomy flat in Wilmersdorf, Berlin. Right in the middle of Berlin with magnificent large trees shading the streets. Like most apartments, it had a room for a maid, which was customary. Growing up, I was told that I was an adorable little girl, endowed with a sunny disposition, big brown eyes, and dark hair. My grandfather, Dad, and I, all had brown eyes, while the rest of the family had blue eyes. It made me sad that I did not inherit blue eyes like the rest of my family. I never grew up to be very tall because of the absence of food and vitamins after the war. The only vitamin we had was Lebertran, a horrible-tasting concoction made from fish. Both my father and mother were taller, but I remained the same height, as most of my closest girlfriends in the Eastern Zone under Russian occupancy.

One summer, my father decided to send my mother on vacation to the Baltic Sea. Soon after her return, my father and his friend visited a swimming facility in Berlin which was closed. Upon returning to his flat, he found his wife in bed with another man (called 'Kurschatten' or Spa Shadow), whom she picked up while visiting the seaside resort. It ended up in a bitter divorce, with my father claiming custody of me, to the utter joy of my grandmother. At the age of three, I was motherless.

Since my mother was not capable of providing for herself, Dad suggested she would learn typing and stenography, so she could earn her money. Of course, none of this ever happened with my mother, who, according to her and the times they lived in, believed to be taken care of by a man. She grew up spoiled and was told by her mother she was the prettiest of the four in her family.

1935, my Mom with me at the beach in Prerow. They called me Püppi (little doll)

Dad and I in Zoppot at the beach with bear

Grandma and I at Bansin beach

Bertha, our wonderful loving housekeeper, took over our household. She was a great and inventive cook. Bertha was a young woman, who came from the Sudetenland in the Eastern part of Europe and had a little girl out of wedlock whom her grandparents were raising. I remember breakfast with cream of wheat with butter and brown sugar, famous German Rouladen, and strawberry pies on my June birthdays. In the fall, our famous German fresh Italian prune cakes. After my mother was gone, I sleepwalked and would wake up screaming, sending my father and Bertha to my rescue.

House Keeper Bertha and I in Kleinmachnow

1940, house keeper Bertha and I ready for first grade

I spent weekends with my grandmother in Steglitz. She would save old bread to feed the ducks and swans in the neighboring park. I ate most of the bread before we reached the animals because I liked it. We also would visit the famous Berlin Zoo on weekends, where my favorite animals were the monkeys.

My grandmother made delicious green salads with seven herbs, which were of importance to her, and they were an essential addition to her wonderful fresh green salads.

I remember as well a man coming through the streets with his barrel organ (Leierkasten) for which a famous song had been composed "Lieber Leierkastenmann….." Quite often a little monkey, all dressed up and so cute, would sit on one side of his organ.

On one occasion, Bertha served very salty ham for dinner (dinner in Germany is served around noon). Since I had to finish my plate and hated ham, I kept it chewed up and deposited inside both sides of my cheeks, looking like a little hamster. Dad and his guests decided to take a ride in his new automobile and myself with the ham inside both cheeks. When we returned from this trip, I still had this mass of ham in both of my cheeks. I can't remember if I had to swallow it or if I was allowed to spit it out.

We spent our summer vacations on the Baltic Sea (in Germany called the Ostsee-East Sea), traveling by train, either to Zoppot, Bansin, Prerow, Zingst, and Binz. One time, when Dad talked too long with another lady, I took off with my big white blown-up swan and headed towards the beach. In panic, Dad asked everyone if they had seen a little girl with a white swan tucked under her arm. I still have a photo taken with Dad and myself, and a man dressed as an ice bear, standing behind us and someone taking a photo. My grandmother made me wear dresses so I wouldn't get sunburned. I hated that.

We stayed in fishermen's cottages, which were quite rustic. Bertha, of course, accompanied us. I remember sailboat trips with tasty smoked fish on rolls. I loved these fish rolls.

At the Baltic Sea, harmless jellyfish occasionally swam close to us. The kids would play with them, which scared me. I refused to swim when these little monster jellyfish were around. Dad would visit friends, take me along, and leave me in strange places. I hated being left by him, which made me feel insecure.

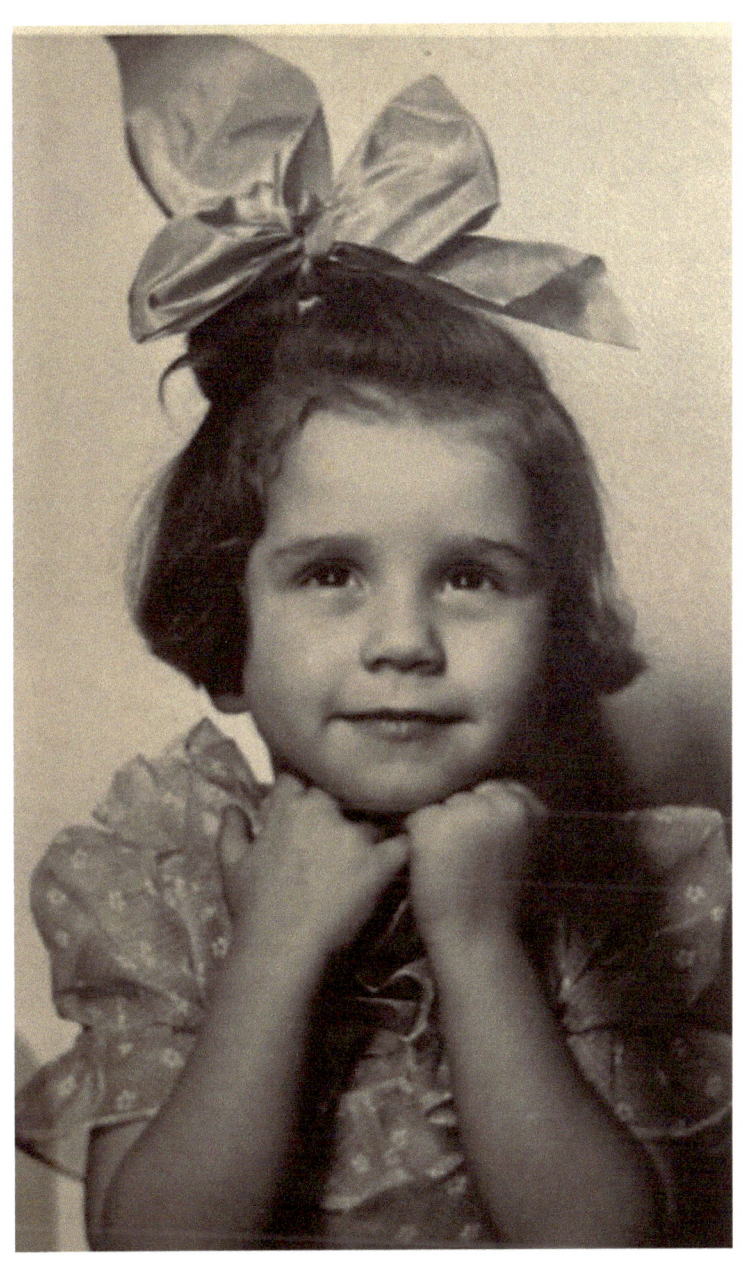

5 year old, taken in Berlin for my Dad's birthday

Plenty of presents were given to me by Dad's clients, like beautiful big dolls with real hair, teddies, and scrumptious fancy chocolates. These chocolates were mostly eaten by my grandmother, who would tell me, *"Children do not appreciate such fine things."* She replaced them with ordinary chocolates.

One day, an uncle visited and brought along his terrier. This terrier had an evil temper and attacked me, which made me jump up on a desk screaming, and my poor uncle had problems controlling his barking dog. Although I loved animals and dogs my entire life, this poor soul had to be put down because of his foul temper and aggressiveness.

I very much enjoyed the years before World War II began. Our lives would never be the same as they were after this maniac with his henchmen took over our beautiful country of famous poets, writers, and composers. Before the war, every morning, fresh, crisp rolls would hang in a bag on the front door of our apartment, together with a large glass of yogurt and a bottle of milk.

Dad would take me to his exclusive tennis club at the Wannsee Lake in Berlin where I learned how to swim. When I turned four, we took a skiing trip to Cortina d'Ampezzo, a ritzy ski resort, where my grandmother and I learned to ski under the guidance of a ski instructor. Every time we went skiing Dad would hire a ski instructor. That introduced me to a sport I loved the most, together with Dad and later on with my son. We stayed in a very exclusive hotel. Every day, an adorable little Italian boy would knock at our door and pick me up for dinner time. At Christmas time, we children danced around a beautifully decorated tree, which reached to the top of the high ceiling. One evening, we managed to topple this tree, but it was caught in time by the personnel.

1938, four years old, skiing in Cortina d'Ampezzo, Italy

Skiing in the Karpaten, Poland

At the age of five, I was enrolled in kindergarten. I remember those days were not too pleasant. I must have talked too much, probably being an only child and having no siblings. As punishment, I ended up with tape on my mouth and had to stand in a corner. We all walked home alone or in groups, and a rumor spread among us children about a man in his yard around the corner, who was watching us walk by, that he was a monster who ate little kids. He was just a harmless old man who enjoyed seeing us children. The adults would teach us not to go with strange uncles who would offer us candies. I played the usual games kids play, with the neighbor kids – hopscotch, rope jumping, hide and seek, and marbles. Rope jumping was my favorite, and I showed enormous endurance. As little girls, we liked to play with our paper dolls, which we cut out and redressed a thousand times.

One of our daily highlights was to sneak into the back doors of a movie house right next door to our building after people left the cinema, but we were thrown out every time by the personnel as soon as the movie theatre filled up with customers. Below our apartment house lay a small park with beautiful tall trees. What I also remember and what impressed me were the Litfaßsäulen (cylinder-shaped advertising pillars), which became very popular throughout Europe. The purpose was, one could paste and display advertising on them with the latest news about theatres and opera, together with Nazi propaganda hate pamphlets. In 1855 were the first ones erected, and their inventor was the printer Ernst Litfaß. I recall seeing the hideous drawn face of a Jewish person to warn the population. I also saw a poster with the warning, "Beware, the enemy is listening!" (Vorsicht, Feind hört mit).

Since I had a curvature of the spine, I was enrolled in gymnastics. One day, at about the age of five years, they let me walk by myself to the large main street bustling with cars. I tucked on the jacket of a trustworthy-looking policeman and asked him, *"Dear uncle policeman, would you please take me across the street?"* It must have been adorable to have this little girl in her little voice ask this kind man for help. He did so, took me by my little hand, and walked me across while all cars stopped. He also waited on the other side, until I returned from my gymnastics session, to guide me back across. I was taught to show respect towards the police and act politely.

Just before I was schooled into first grade, I came down with measles and mumps. It meant spending time in my bed in a darkened room for a few weeks and in utter boredom. When the doctor finally allowed me to visit the grade school, I received a large paper cone filled with chocolates and candies and a Rantzen (backpack) with my slate, chalk, and crayons.

Great value was placed in school for proper spelling, proper handwriting, and reading. A photo was taken of Bertha, our housekeeper, and me, with my daily bow in my hair.

November 9, 1938

The synagogues burned, and the firemen did nothing to quelch the flames. Prior to that time, all Jewish people had been declared 'non-citizens.' That night, many of them were beaten, incarcerated, killed, and placed in concentration camps. Books were burned and famous writers were denounced, including Dad's friend, the writer Erich Kästner.

The following day, Bertha and I visited the small shop down below to the left in our apartment building, where the kind store lady put some candy into my little hand. When we left the store Bertha slapped my hand and told me, *"You do not accept candy from Jews."* I felt it was terribly unjust. I did not ask her why, nor did I pay attention if the glass front of the store had been smashed and "Jude" smeared on the broken glass front.

1939

Hitler declared war on Poland. Warsaw suffered heavy air attacks and artillery by the Germans. Racial annihilation was carried out by Hitler's henchmen with the greatest brutality and without mercy by his Einsatzgruppen (Mobil Killing Units). Jewish people were crammed into the famous Ghetto of Warsaw, and Intelligenza was shot in a famous Polish forest - terrible consequences for the people of Poland and the citizens of Warsaw.

Times for the German population would change as well for the worse.

Hitler declared, *"Canons instead of butter."* Everyone had rationing cards for food, gasoline, and clothing - no more oranges, bananas, or southern fruits. I remember how my last overripe banana tasted so good. Life went on as usual. In school, we stood up when the teacher entered the class, and we were made to raise our right arm and shout "Heil Hitler" or at demonstrations when the Nazis paraded through the streets. I did not ever remember seeing Hitler. I only remember when raising my right arm, it would start hurting and I would support my right arm with my left arm. I was reprimanded harshly for that.

After Hitler overran Poland, he annexed 1938/1939 The Federal States of Austria, Sudetenland, Moravia, Silesia, Bohemia, and the Czechoslovak Republic, wherever German-speaking folks had lived for centuries.

The Nazis had carefully planned all of that before Chamberlain met with Hitler on September 30, 1938, and then returned to England declaring to his people, "Peace for our time."

Shortly before the war ended, Dad and I returned to Berlin one more time to see that this magnificent and beautiful city lay in rubble and ashes after severe Allied bombings. No street would be recognized. It left a sore and everlasting impression on me.

*NAZI GERMANY AND ANTI-JEWISH POLICY

The Nazi Party rose to power with an anti-Semitic racial ideology. However, the anti-Jewish campaign was not conducted according to a blueprint, rather, it evolved. Before the outbreak of the war, political and economic factors, as well as public opinion both inside and outside Germany, influenced the evolution of Nazi anti-Jewish laws and measures.

The main purpose of the anti-Jewish policy between 1933 and 1939, according to the racial theory, was to isolate German Jewry from German society. These laws sought to uproot and dispossess Jews economically from daily life in Germany and encourage them to leave their homeland. These laws limited and humiliated Jews on a daily basis.

(1933-1939) Divided into Three Periods:

- The first period, 1933-1934, included boycotts against Jews and the Civil Service Law that dismissed Jews from government jobs.

- The second period began in the spring of 1935 and was marked by the establishment of the racially based Nuremberg Laws. Jews were no longer German citizens.

- The third period from 1937–1939 was a time of increasing anti-Jewish violence, confiscation of Jewish property, and forbidding Jewish ownership of business concerns. The turning point of this period was the Kristallnacht Pogrom.

Anti-Jewish Policy by Year

1933

-All non-Aryans were dismissed from holding government jobs. This regulation applied to public school teachers, university professors, doctors, lawyers, engineers, etc. – all Jews who held government positions of any kind. Non-Aryans were defined as Jews, the children of Jews, and the grandchildren of Jews.

- A general boycott of all Jewish-owned businesses was proclaimed. Officially it lasted for one day, but actually, it continued for much longer in many locations.

- Membership in the Reich Chamber of Culture was prohibited. This meant that Jews could not hold jobs in radio, in the theaters, or sell paintings or sculptures.

- Mass bonfires were ignited throughout Germany. Books written by Jews and anti-Nazis were burned. Jews were prohibited from owning land.

- Jewish lawyers and judges were barred from their professions. Jewish doctors were barred from treating "Aryan" patients.

- Jews were prohibited from producing kosher meat.

1935

- The Reichstag (government) adopted the Nuremberg Laws, which declared that Jews could no longer be citizens of Germany.

- Marriage and intimate relations between Jews and those of "Aryan" blood were declared criminal acts.

- German females under the age of 45 were prohibited from being employed by Jews.

- Jews were forbidden to wave the Reich's flag or to display the flag's colors.

1936

- Hitler temporarily relaxed the anti-Semitic propaganda and other measures against Jews in order to avoid criticism by foreign visitors attending the Summer Olympic Games in Berlin.

1937

- "Aryanization," the confiscation of Jewish businesses and property, intensified greatly.

1938

- The Reich Supreme Court declared that being a Jew was cause for dismissal from a job.

- The Nuremberg Laws were extended to Austria after the Anschluss, the annexation of Austria.

- All Jews had to add the names "Israel" and "Sarah" to their identification papers, and passports were marked with the "red letter J," for Jude (Jew).

- Jews could no longer attend plays and concerts, own phones, or have driver's licenses, car registrations, etc.

- Kristallnacht Pogrom (Night of Broken Glass): approximately 1,400 synagogues were burned, 7,000 stores owned by Jews and hundreds of homes were damaged and looted.

- 30,000 Jews, most of them leaders in the Jewish communities, were sent to concentration camps. Many were offered the opportunity to leave the camps provided they could prove they had arranged their emigration from Germany.

- Very few Jewish children remained in German schools.

- All Jewish shops were ordered to close by December 31, 1938.

- Jews had to abide by curfews.

Between 1933 and 1938, nearly 150,000 Jews managed to leave Nazi Germany. This number represented approximately 30 percent of the total Jewish population. In order for Jews to legally emigrate from Germany, they were required to have both German passports and visas permitting them to enter another country. Most countries, however, had quotas that limited the number of immigrants allowed to enter and required that those entering were able to support themselves. Very few countries admitted German-Jewish refugees and after the *Kristallnacht Pogrom*, it became extremely difficult for Jews to leave Germany. Most of the Jews who fled Germany went to other European countries that were occupied by the Nazis months or a few years later."

*(Adapted with permission from Echoes and Reflections, 2005 Anti-Defamation League, USC Shoah Foundation, Yad Vashem www.echoesandreflections.org (All rights reserved).

I learned that 'pets' were forbidden to be owned by Jewish citizens, and had to be left behind when their owners left. It must have been heart-wrenching for the children to have to part from their beloved pets. Taken into consideration, these were our citizens and wonderful people who would be deprived of their homeland and their possessions, whose fathers and sons had fought and died for their Fatherland during World War I. Later in life, it was sad and awful for me to learn about these atrocities. What humans are capable of? All humans should be treated with respect and understanding, including animals and nature. All of this weighed me down and depressed me. It is known that throughout centuries, people have persecuted Jewish citizens. I learned about these crimes after the war was over. Ever since that time, I have been busy educating myself about history. The Holocaust was real! Mankind has to accept these facts. THERE IS NO DENIAL! I grew up with these horrors, and my family confirmed all the stories after the war. These wonderful citizens were the heart of our society, brilliant, inventive, and ambitious, but causing enormous envy among the ordinary citizens, who feared for their positions in government and industry. Dad always said after the war, *"Hitler killed our Intelligenza."*

*On January 20, 1942 - Fifteen high-ranking Nazi Party and German government officials gathered at a villa in the Berlin suburb of Wannsee to discuss and coordinate the implementation of what they called "The Final Solution of the Jewish Question." (mass killing). The SS envisioned that some 11 million Jews, some of them not living on German-controlled territory, would be eradicated as part of the Nazi program."

Holocaust Encyclopedia

1939 – 1940 Poland

On September 1, 1939, after Germany invaded Poland, the Soviet Union invaded Poland from the East. Polish groups formed partisans. Since the Nazis thirsted for living space and considered the Polish people among other nations as "inferior," Nazi Germany decided to bomb and invade Poland, together with the Soviets, under a non-aggression pact. By the year 1940, Warsaw had fallen to the Nazis. However, on June 22, 1941, this Union ended when Nazi Germany launched a surprise attack against the Soviet Union, its former ally in the war against Poland. Prior to that, the Nazis already had taken France, Belgium, and Holland with Blitz Attack actions.

Besides other unbelievable horror scenarios executed by the Nazis (SS) are two very important events that took place: "The heinous massacres around the village of Wilka Piasnica, Poland, where mass executions were carried out in the woods by the SS between the fall and spring of 1940. The Palmiry Massacre where the Polish political, cultural, and social elite were taken from their beds in the middle of the night and murdered. This was documented on June 21, 1940. Inside the Ghetto, Jewish people lived under horrible circumstances in cramped quarters starving and freezing to death.

The time came when Dad was commissioned by the German government to relocate to Warsaw. The Polish people needed assistance with their problems and few German attorneys were available. Dad purchased a Diplomat Flat, where Polish people lived in the back of this apartment complex, divided by a small park. He opened his law practice to negotiate between the Nazis and the Polish people. A roomy flat was located on the upper floors of an apartment complex where other Germans lived. The apartment house had marble stairs and walls and an elevator.

When entering the entrance door to the flat it opened into a small hallway. To the left was a tiny room where the Polish butler sat who greeted the clients. And a small balcony overlooking a green area with tall trees and housing for the Polish people. At the end of the hallway to the right was a large vestibule, from which were left the living/dining room, a large storage room with a refrigerator, and a kitchen with two sinks, and behind the kitchen the maid's quarter. Ahead of the vestibule through a door, a large room opened up that seated the Polish bookkeeper with two secretaries. To the right of the vestibule, a door led into my father's domain, furnished with a heavy secretary facing the window, a Chippendale sofa with three comfortable big chairs with a round table. On the wall of his office hung a large portrait of myself as a little girl, with a large bow in my hair, sitting on a small stool, dressed in a white dress and holding a doll. Next to the left hung our family Crest, which I remember had big feathers with other ornaments. There was a door in the secretary and bookkeeper's room as well that led into my father's office. My stepmother did not save the painting and the Crest, the day she decided to ship our furniture by trucks towards Rinteln a.d. Weser (later West Germany), shortly before the Russians invaded Poland.

To the very right of the vestibule was another long hallway, with rooms left and right, filled with personnel and another attorney. (I would meet this attorney and his wife again after the war when I lived in the United States. They told me that they felt so sorry for me because of the way I was treated by my stepmother that they planned to adopt me).

At the end of that long narrow hallway to the left were two rooms preserved for my father and I. A long balcony ran along both of our bedrooms. I loved to play on the balcony, work in the dirt - plant and replant. The outdoors became one of my favorite hobbies. I never was a city girl and much later would find out the reason behind my unusual behavior.

My room was furnished with a bed, furniture, dolls, teddies, and a tall toy blackboard. I also had a toy shop with artificial groceries. Every day, I placed my dolls and teddies in rows in front of the blackboard and pretended to be a teacher. People who knew me assumed I would someday choose that as my profession. I diligently combed my beautiful dolls' real hair every day. I possessed a small baby buggy in which I later transported my dog, 'bless his patient soul,' to cart him around the flat. Shortly after that, I was placed into a German grade school and Bertha brought me to school and picked me up. I can't remember anything about that school.

Instead of Zloty (Polish money), Dad's Polish clients often compensated Dad with beautiful and intricate carved wooden gifts, also once with a very large crossbow. There were buckets with meats and living carp swimming in the two roomy sinks in the kitchen. Later, Polly, our replacement for Bertha, would let me help bake and cook, and I was an eager companion in her kitchen.

We would meet in the dining room for meals, and I would complete my studies in the living room, by rummaging through a small library next to it.

One day, my stepmother unexpectedly entered the living/dining room area. I hastily put an ink mark on the side of the adult book I was reading, not wanting her to know I had read one of her books. Later on, she discovered the ink spot and questioned how this ink mark had gotten into her book. She never found out. We also had a complete set of German Encyclopedia. I was fascinated by the human autonomy in which one could unfold parts of female and male organs.

Long after bedtime at night, Dad would come into my room and bid me 'good night,' which would not keep me from using a flashlight under my big featherbed to read my books in secret.

Before my stepmother entered our lives, I would spend my days with school, visiting friends, my dolls, teddies, and reading, and being quite content, not to count the skiing and beach trips with Dad, my grandmother, and Bertha. There were nights I became restless and left my bedroom through the front door and headed downstairs. They retrieved me. I was scolded and often spanked hard. Child psychology was unknown to them.

One winter day, Dad and his friends decided to take a sleigh ride in a comfortable sleigh for six people, pulled by two sturdy, warm-blooded horses. We were covered with fur blankets and bundled up to stay cozy and warm. At one point, the adults decided to put me on a child's sleigh and connect me with a strong cord to the back of their big sleigh. They did not realize they lost me on the snow-packed path deep in the woods. There I sat, severed from the big sleigh, all by myself in the middle of a lonely road in the woods, thinking of wolves coming to get me. By the time the adults realized I had been lost, they found me in tears and scared to death.

My Dad had a good friend by the name of Paul von Dimetrenko, who was a native of the Ukraine, which by then was occupied by the Nazis. I remember the "Borscht" soup we ate and two paintings he gave to Dad, together with a very big beautiful doll with real hair. One of these paintings is still in my possession, while the other one was given to a relative. Both are by a famous Ukrainian painter.

1942

When I nearly reached the age of eight, one day my thirty-seven-year-old Dad presented me with a new mother, age twenty-two, whom he met and married in Berlin. It satisfied my grandmother, who felt her son had led a rather sleazy life with women. There was a secret staircase leading off the corridor across from our bedrooms. It was rumored, that Dad kept another apartment down below where he received his lovers. I met his new wife and was told, *"Say Mom to her; she now is your new mother."* When I curtseyed and held out my little hand to shake hers, I realized I never would warm up to her. Over the years I got to know her, I would neither trust nor like her.

An aunt told me later that my stepmother was extremely jealous of me.

She was quite pretty, her dark hair colored blond, with brown eyes. Hitler's ideal was people with blue eyes and blond hair, a straight nose, and a high forehead. My stepmother made sure I was aware of this. She was a great admirer of Hitler. One time she marched in the 1936 Olympics in Berlin where she shook Hitler's hand. She told me, *"When Hitler shook my hand, I would not wash my hand for an entire week."* (Stupid woman)

She was of medium height with her hair fashioned in a way ladies wore their hairdos and clothing in those days. An air of coldness emitted from her. Her name was Uschi. She later would say, *"I was not aware your father had a child."* Her wonderful, gentle mother from Berlin told me the opposite.

"She knew very well she married a man with a child." Her mother, whom I called Omi, was a mild-mannered lady to whom I became very attached. Omi taught me how to use a certain sewing stitch for a seam, which I use to this day. Unfortunately, she was too meek to stand up to her rather resolute daughter. I think she was afraid of her. From what I gathered, Uschi inherited her deceased father's strong and nasty character, who had worked in the government. Omi was widowed and lived with a lady friend in Berlin. They shared an apartment. From time to time, she would visit us in Warsaw.

Her daughter Uschi was very ambitious and possessed by immense wickedness and cruelty, and it delighted her to torture me. Since she despised children, she would torment me with terrible stories about my mother, the way I looked, or the way I acted. One kind thing she did was purchase a terrier puppy by the name of Jerry. To her dismay, this dog would bond with me forever rather than with her. When they fled Warsaw from the Russians, they lost my precious Jerry. I was inconsolable and cried for years. My grandmother did not like animals, and I would not own a dog until I left Germany and married. But I still have his photo. My father also gave me two turtles, which I pampered with lettuce and food. They were kept on the small balcony overlooking the park-like area where the Polish people lived. I loved those little guys. They would stick their heads out to greet me. One day they disappeared. I hate to think what their fate might have been.

1942, my beloved dog Jerry in Warsaw

One time Dad's bedroom was open, and I discovered two bowls filled with candies. I grabbed as much candy as I could carry and stuffed them into my apron pockets, then headed towards the little balcony by the front door. I called the Polish children and threw the candies down to them. What a glorious moment! When my stepmother discovered this, there was trouble and the room stayed locked for the rest of the entire time we lived in Warsaw. Since I was brought up that storks bring the babies and I longed for a little sister or brother, they told me to put sugar lumps on the windowsill and the stork would get them.

My father was called into the German Army when the war neared its end in Warsaw, but only as a Private. One day, someone took me to the movies to watch Nazi propaganda news that showed the fighting of German soldiers and their enormous successes. I began to cry bitterly afraid Dad could be killed. He was a man who never learned to shoot a gun and looked ridiculous in his army uniform. I gave him a talisman, a tiny black metal teddy, which is a symbol of protection. I still have it and I carry it around in my purse.

Every morning, when he knocked on my door and discovered that I had allowed Jerry to sleep at the foot of my bed to warm my feet, he would spank me unmercifully. This lasted for weeks and became a ritual. The first time, Jerry ripped Dad's pants to defend me, so my father kicked him into the hallway. I screamed, and Jerry barked - quite a scenario. My father was good at punishing me, which was an old disciplinary Prussian way. I never would lay hands on my son. A child should never be beaten – a 'no' to "don't spare the rod" attitude.

Prior to all of this, the first thing my stepmother did was fire Bertha, my trusted friend and substitute mom, for years. From afar, Bertha watched over me. One day, our well-endowed Polish housekeeper, Polly, said to me before I left for grade school, *"Child, I am sorry your stepmother locked the fridge. I will have to spread jam on your lunch sandwich."* My stepmother was notorious for carrying keys around by the dozen and locking every piece of furniture or door she could find. Shortly after that, the Polish secretary whispered to me, *"Bertha sent you a care package."* Of course, the bread hardened over time, and the cold cuts did not keep in the secretary's desk drawers for long.

After the war, Dad tried to locate Bertha, but to no avail. We think either she with her family were killed or must have fled. Bertha and her family lost their beautiful home and farm in Sudetenland, a mountainous area in Yugoslavia, to join in the long line of refugees. Bertha took me to her home one time. It was a stately farmhouse with a low-hanging thatched roof surrounded by lush green acreage. I heard a shot in the morning, and for dinner, we had roasted hare on the table. Her brothers had been busy hunting early in the morning. I remember that time vividly because it gave me a feeling of home, love, and family. I felt quite honored to be brought to her family home. Customarily, the entire family of mother, father, brothers, and whoever else lived under one roof.

The next step, my stepmother booted me out of my room in Warsaw, which was next to Dad's bedroom, by placing my bed in that little cubbyhole by the front door, together with the butler. I was only allowed to play in my old room next to Dad's bedroom but not sleep there. Whenever I got sick and I came down with Scarlet Fever, I would look out at the dreary grey roofs with their ugly chimneys and dream of meadows with flowers and trees. I was so sick that I ended up in the hospital, in a room tiled up to the ceiling in white, secured behind glass walls. Dad came every day! He was my only visitor.

I would have terrible fever nightmares. After they brought me back home into my little cubbyhole, the doctors worried I might have Diphtheria, which is a very serious disease. So, one day, I was injected with two huge needles into my behind. I screamed. To this day I hate needles. Because of all the neglect and parental love, I fell sick quite often, more likely to gain attention.

One of my little girlfriends lost her dad through Polish partisans. Retribution! For revenge, twenty innocent Polish citizens would be arrested on their way to work, placed against the wall of any house, and immediately shot by the SS. Our nice bookkeeper, the dad of three children, was apprehended by the SS on the way to Dad's office and shot. I heard the commotion and how my father tried to save him. That would be Nazi retaliation for German officers who were murdered by the partisans. It hurt me because he was so kind to me; so was our butler, who shared his meager sandwich with my dog Jerry: such sweet, wonderful people - all gone. I remember reading later that my Uncle Harry von Rosen wrote in his memoirs that Dad saved several Jewish people from their deaths.

I remember driving in a car and being told that to the left was the Ghetto, where the Jewish people were forced to live. Oblivious to what happened around me, I knew nothing when I grew up. I recall that Dad took me on trips long before he remarried walking through meadows close to woods, when a group of Polish children came to greet us and offered us sweet-smelling wild strawberries in their open hands. It seems they only grow in Europe. Their perfume scent is beguiling and has become one of my favorites among strawberries. They are rather small in appearance. The remembrance of such a sweet gesture by these children lingers with me until today. That night, Dad and I found lodging in an old farmhouse, where I discovered bugs running up and down the wall. *"Look Dad ladybugs."* Dad burst out laughing and told everyone later that I mistakenly took cockroaches for ladybugs.

Before my stepmother came into our life, life was peaceful and safe. After that, uniformed officers and dignities would visit Dad at night, acting boisterous and drunk. They most likely could not stand themselves being murderers. Unbelievable, family fathers, with wives and children - where was their conscience?

Prior to Dad's remarriage, I spent time with Dad and my grandmother on skiing trips, in beautiful places like Krynica in the Karpaten mountains in Poland. On one occasion, Dad and I were snowed in for two weeks on a train. The snow was so high they could not move the train. It was an adventure for me since Dad and I had a sleeper cabin with two comfortable bunk beds and plenty of food in their dining room. How I treasured these moments, these weeks I had Dad all to myself. He was a jolly fun-loving dad, with a great sense of humor, which I fortunately inherited from him. All of that fun stopped abruptly when he remarried. My grandmother wrote in her memoirs, *"Finally, Horst found a mother for our little girl!"*

***Berlin 1942, Wedding between Ursula Weit and
Dr. Horst Ganske, my Dad***

I remember one day visiting the beautiful "Tuchhalle" (cloth hall) Arcades in Cracow, from where two exquisite rod iron plates still adorn my walls. I would never get over this empty feeling of not having a real mother, which made me retreat into my world of books, where books were my preferred gifts and I asked for them on birthdays and holidays. I loved fairytales and Bertha would read them to me every night, but they also caused nightmares. I have read them all – Danish, Northern Sagas, British fairytales, French, German, you name it. Dad would tell me, *"You are my fairytale aunt."* I would quote passages from fairytales to him. History also was one of my favorites.

One summer day, Dad took me to a Rittergut. Rittergüter were enormous ranches owned by people with large German land holdings, forestry, and breeding of beautiful Trakena horses. Land of moose roaming about. Danzig, the capital, at the time it belonged to Prussia, is now called Gedansk. This ranch had a beautiful manor, cool and mysterious inside, furnished with heavy carpets and massive furniture. The couple and their kids were very nice to me. I remember stepping on a bee. The pain was lasting and uncomfortable. The property had a large lake below the mansion with ducks and swans on it. With a fenced yard growing gorgeous tall dahlias, sunflowers, and vegetables. It was a beautiful, peaceful place to live. After that summer vacation, I decided I wanted to marry a man who owned a Prussian Ranch and have five children with him. Later in life, my grandmother told me that she knew a lady who had seven sons. She endowed each of her sons with a Prussian Ranch. All of that was lost after the war. People had to flee and leave their beautiful places and their animals, together with all of their belongings. The result of Nazi dictatorship. Thank you, Hitler!

There was another time I was invited to spend Christmas with a wealthy rancher's family. We were surprised by Santa Claus dressed up like a Bishop, in a long white gown with his tall miter (headdress) and walking with a long golden bishop's staff. Krampus accompanied him, a creature with a hideously ugly face mask who spanks and reprimands naughty children. We children were quite intimidated, but later to find these clothes in some living room drawers.

One day, a young guest visited us in Warsaw. She was the daughter of General Behrendt. He fought alongside General Fieldmarschall Rommel in North Africa. I noticed she was allowed to leave food on her plate. She was tall and thin as a beanstalk, but picky. I complained, only to be told it was the way it was, period! I had to clean up my plate.

When we had our breakfast and capped our hard-boiled eggs, I would finish first; then, after Dad would finish, I would turn the eggshell upside down. I offered him my empty egg and he would accept it as a joke. He would roar up and chase me around the dining room table to the utter dislike and complaints of my stepmother. I would scream and laugh. It was a ritual and our game. One time Dad put on a gasmask and chased me around the flat until I started to cry and begged him that it scared me to death. He apologized.

They often were gone at night. When they left, I would find some silly gown, place planks between the office tables, stand on them, and sing operas at the top of my voice. I imagined I would be an opera singer since I really had a very good soprano in those days. To top this, I would take boxes of paper clips and lock them together until I had strings of them a mile long. The poor personnel the next day had to try to untangle this mess. Nothing was ever said. Wonderful people!

Operetta Gräfin Marizza, I am top left, first girl, on the roof of the Opera

The Nazis demanded that all Aryan children at the age of six should join their Hitler Youth programs of BDM (Bund Deutscher Mädel).

Dad was asked repeatedly when he would have me join. Dad refused. I never belonged to any such group.

The war was not ending well as the Nazis had planned. As I learned later in life, on January 20, 1942, the Wannsee Conference in Berlin was held, where high-ranking German officials gathered with the "Final Solution of the Jewish Population." Total annihilation of all Jews and unwanted people.

April 19, 1943

The Jewish Ghetto Uprising began in Warsaw. The Nazi regime razed the city by trying to remove the last Jewish people using flame throwers by destroying houses and historical buildings. The Russians did not help as planned. But from May 4 and 5, 1943, the Soviets bombed Warsaw, and air raid alarms sounded over Warsaw. We escaped into air raid cellars, leaving everything behind but carrying our small emergency suitcase. The minute Russian bombers flew over us, one could see bright searchlights up in the sky looking for Russian enemy planes. Falling bombs made a high-pitched piping noise with a loud detonation.

Finally, the Blockwart would give the allowance to leave the air raid shelters after the alarms sounded off an all-clear signal with a shrill sound. It sounded loud and threatening. From heavy artillery and bombs, windows burst under air pressure. My beloved dog, Jerry, was not allowed in the air raid cellars. Dad and my stepmother decided that she and I would leave Warsaw and the furniture would be taken in truckloads out of Warsaw to Rinteln a.d. Weser in the West of Germany, which was occupied by Britain after the war. Uschi did not include the painting of me and our family Crest. First, she deposited me somewhere in the State of Thuringia and dropped me off at a small logging place. I only was allowed to bring a backpack (Rucksack). Hastily thrown together were some clothing without my beloved white teddy and my dog.

1945

The Soviets reached and entered Warsaw after the German Army had cleansed the city and turned it into rubble. Fryderyk Chopin's heart, upon his wish, rested in the main cathedral. Warsaw looked like Berlin and the other cities in Germany after the war. A friend of Dad's visited our flat – everything was intact and peaceful. My dolls and teddies still sat in rows in front of the blackboard; the painting and the Crest must have been there as well.

After my stepmother dropped me off, she left. I remember the small farm in Thuringia, with an adjacent logging village. I was a scared and shy little girl without Dad, thrown into the midst of strangers. They were kind farm folk and shared their meager food rations with me. A large slice of dark German bread was served to each of us in the evening, with one fried egg spread over it. Most foods came from their garden and the animals they kept. That winter was bitter cold. The little bedroom I slept in had iced-up windows, creating beautiful ornamental flowers. Staring at the designs stimulated my imagination. It also had an enormously huge featherbed with a giant feather pillow. To keep our feet warm, bricks were heated and wrapped in towels.

Our bedrooms were ice cold, and it was comfy to slip under this huge feather comforter as high and round as a mound of clouds, warming one's feet on the wrapped hot stone. None of the remaining rooms were heated in the farmhouse; only the family kitchen was fed coal or wood into a gigantic cooking stove. The family ate and lived in this roomy atmosphere. The coming summer, the kids caught Forellen (trout) in a narrow stream in front of their house, catching them with their bare hands. We, the children, would romp around the beautiful forests, picking blueberries, raspberries, and wild strawberries. We played between stacked lumber logs in a nearby lumber yard, which was forbidden because of the danger the stacked logs could collapse. We did not give a hoot. One day, my stepmother showed up and Dad arrived on a dilapidated bike. He was dressed in a tuxedo with the tails flying behind him. He looked ridiculous and quite funny. Both had left Warsaw together in their Opel Kadett car, but on that ride, my dog jumped out and got lost.

After dropping me off, Dad must have been summoned back into his unit, then fled on this ridiculous-looking bike. Law and order fell apart and the Russians were advancing from the East. Later, I was told the story that my stepmother had an abortion on her way from Warsaw, which caused her early death of ovarian cancer. She died at the age of forty-four.

I was heartbroken over the loss of my dog. I cried for three years. His photo is still in one of my albums. My grandmother did not like dogs. She would tell me, *"Child, don't let them lick you; they have worms."* In fact, I don't remember that grandmother ever liked any animals. I would not have a dog until I got married.

One sunny day, I was taken by my stepmother to my grandmother in Thuringia. That was shortly before the war ended. Dad and my stepmother relocated as refugees to Deckbergen, close to Rinteln an der Weser. Under the refugee law, residents were forced to give up space in their homes. Dad and my stepmother were allowed one room. These misplaced German refugees caused problems among residents and only too often were called, *"The dirty Eastern pack."* Dad did not have those problems. As an attorney, he was well-liked and even started a small trading business. The same with the Allies. They won the war and felt entitled to take up quarters in private mansions and wherever they chose. After leaving Berlin, my grandmother settled close to her two brothers in Altenburg, Thuringia. I arrived there and felt devastated to have lost my home with all of my precious belongings.

1945

In Thuringia, we waited and feared the end of the war. The end could be ugly. Hitler and his thugs were so desperate that they executed anyone who fled the ranks or refused to fight. The SS (Schutzstaffel or protection squads) were the elite among his troops, and they allowed themselves unbelievable atrocities towards humanity. In the end, they summoned old men and very young boys to take up arms against the enemy. Those who deserted (Fahnenflucht) were hung or shot immediately. There is proof of it. I saw the place where several sixteen-year-old boys were executed by hanging in the State of Bavaria, and now there is a plaque in their memory. After the surrender, everyone destroyed their memorials of Hitler the best they could and hung white sheets from their windows, indicating that they were not the enemy and that they were surrendering.

While living with my grandmother, I was introduced to the opera next door and enrolled as a little ballerina. I had a group of close friends in my ballerina class. There were five of us: Hannelore, Christine, Gigi, and Moni, her sister. One was the daughter of the butcher, the other from the drugstore, and two of them belonged to a well-known publishing company. And how I enjoyed this ballet. I would die for it. There was hardly a day I did not practice. Three of my little girlfriends and I were allowed to appear in the Operetta Countess Maritza, composed by Emmerich Kalman, a Hungarian composer. Dressed up in the cute costumes of the Hungarian folklore, I had the role of singing one line, but as I stepped forward, my voice failed. After a few performances, my grandmother decided, *"Child, it is too late for you, and you are not getting your rest."*

That ended my short career as a singer and actress. But I was allowed to continue with ballet. My girlfriend from the publishing company had a sister. Together we would slip into the costumes of their mother, who had been a well-known concert singer. We dressed up in their basement, prancing around in front of a large standing mirror.

1945

Now to my three cousins – Nicky, four years younger than I, Thomas, and Michael. My Aunt Erika barely made it out of Königsberg i. Prussia when the Russians arrived. She jumped with her three children on the last train out of Kaliningrad (Königsberg) and arrived, to the horror of my grandmother, without any decent clothes. They had to stay with us for some time until my uncle joined later. My uncle never mentioned the war days. He had a white streak on top of his head from a nearly disastrous airline crash. The boys slept in bunkbeds under the roof; my room was right next to theirs. In the morning, since we did not have a toilet on that floor, two buckets were used for toilet needs, and they were filled. It was hard to transport them downstairs to the existing toilet.

In those days, it was customary to own a nightstand with a chamber pot in it, which enabled the sleeper not to visit a bathroom, which often was further from the bedroom.

We had a lot of fun with the old toys from our two dads, which miraculously my grandmother had saved, together with her beautiful blue Meissner Onion china for many guests. Her china and other articles were stored in the attic in very large trunks (after I left, later stolen by refugees who settled in that house). We would build these fabulous Erector Sets, created in 1913 by A.C. Gilbert in the USA. It was extremely popular when Dad and his brother grew up. We also built tents and scrambled around the very steep slated roofs. Had we lost our balance, we would have fallen through the middle of the building. The houses in the old part of Altenburg were built next to each other, very tall and very narrow, like the ones in Amsterdam, Holland. They were built in squares, with an open middle, tall and menacing dark. The sun never reached the bottom of the courtyard.

We also had someone give us a Kasperle Theater made out of wood with a stage, where we children would hold the puppets with our hands under their clothes and act out scenes. Kasperle was the good guy and always won. He rescued the weak and punished the bad. We attracted quite an audience of children who were fascinated to watch the plays. We even tried making a paste from wet newspapers to form heads for our Kasperle Theatre and sew dresses for them. It worked.

Black Peter was another card game, and whoever lost became the Black Peter mustache drawn on his upper mouth, mostly done with soot ashes from the fireplace. There were other card games, but I cannot remember.

I loved playing with my dolls, which I acquired once more from friends.

My relatives loaned us a very beautiful and tall doll house, from another time, exquisitely furnished, with old-fashioned dolls in old-fashioned clothes. My grandmother still had tin toys, which were quite famous in Germany. They were windup toys. Kids loved playing with them. One of them was a dad, and when wound up he would swing his little boy around in circles.

The narrow house we lived in was in an especially old area, not far from a beautiful big castle. It was three stories high, with a shop down below on the left of the building. One entered a dark, cool entrance hall, straight ahead was a steep, narrow staircase leading up to three floors. Past the staircase going upstairs, to the left was a narrow hallway entering into the stony courtyard, from which a door opened into a large washroom. In there were two enormously round vats, which were heated with coal or wood, to boil the white laundry. One of the round vats was for washing the clothes, the other for rinsing them. My grandmother would use a large wooden paddle to swing the washed clothes into the rinsing vat. It must have cost her enormous strength to perform this ritual. The colored clothes were scrubbed on a washboard on a corrugated metallic surface.

The narrow hallway led to a door into the cellar. The walls were constructed in thick layers of stone. At the end of the cellar was a bricked-up wall. It was rumored that a tunnel led right up to the nearby castle where folks when threatened by wars could escape. I wouldn't say I liked going into the cellar and would sing at the top of my voice to cover my fear. We had a room in which, in good times, jams, canned fruits, and vegetables were being kept. It was pitch black down there, and only a flashlight helped. It also would serve as our air-raid cellar towards the end of the war.

My two older cousins and I would sled as often as we could. One time, my older cousin Nicky brushed too close to a tree, which hit and cracked my left ankle. My uncle, the family doctor, looked at it but did nothing. I laid for days on our sofa in our small living room, suffering great pain. I had to get through it by myself. Apparently, they were short of pain meds. I did not forgive them for this and also found them pretty uppish in their behavior.

My grandmother suffered from severe kidney problems and often would moan next door in her small and narrow bedroom, in which at the end stood her piano, from which she never parted. One day, she was operated on and I had to stay with one of my aunts for one week, the wife of my grandmother's brother, the eye doctor. My eye doctor uncle believed, *"People should have 50 grams of butter for the sake of their eyesight."* How well spoken in times when there only was margarine to be had, if ever available.

It was Christmas time, and I imagined I heard Santa Claus up in the sky. I did not care for the lady of the house. She was of a tall angular build and did not make a kind and warm impression on me. I found her distant and cold. She told me, *"My favorite son is missing on the Eastern front, and the other one is still alive but is a prisoner of war. I favor the son who has been declared dead."* That stayed with me forever, and I swore I would never distinguish between my children and love them equally. I was glad to get back to my grandmother, who gave me some sort of security and the feeling of having a home. I had been handed around all my life, and it left its scars.

Also, being an only child affected me to the point that I never really trusted anyone and felt very much alone. It was either sink or swim in my lifetime!

We had the opera just a stone's throw from our house around the corner. My grandmother made sure we would study her little opera booklets which had the text of the opera in it and described the course of events. We went quite often and listened to grand opera. To this day, I am a great friend of opera. On the piano, I could play Mozart, Bach, Beethoven, Brahms, and Grieg, one of my favorites because of his melancholic music.

In the very last war days, the German Army silos opened with their supplies. My grandmother found a small ladder wagon and started towards the silos. When she returned from her adventure, she told me, *"The men were trampling on sugar, flour, sacks of dried goods, and bags busted. There was a shoving and pushing, and I am happy I could fill my little wagon with canned meats."* My grandmother would take her valuable tablecloths, together with her embroidered initialed napkins, on what we called *"walking across the country"* to barter with her treasures and towards the end return with not more than a bowl of fruit or some veggies. (It was customary that when a girl grew up and started her trousseau, silver cutlery would be engraved with her new family's initials. I still have some of those pieces, one from Dad when he was baptized and two spoons with my name engraved on them. My grandmother would talk about grand dinners given in their home at Grandpa's school, with twenty-four guests seated at their table. I asked her how she managed to keep her slim waist, and she answered, *"We only would take very little of the dishes offered, which often were five-course meals since we had servants."*

Before the war ended, we experienced tremendous attacks of Allied airplanes dropping bombs everywhere around us. Altenburg was pretty much spared, but still, there was some damage. The sirens placed on the roofs would howl, and the searchlights would cross the night skies.

One could see the Allied fighter planes coming in troves, dropping the bombs like pearls one after the other. The sounds of swishing, whistling, and crashing of the bombs – afterward total silence! Somewhere, a refinery was burning, and the sky was lit up bright red for weeks. We fled into our makeshift air raid bunker with its thick cellar walls. A Spanish lady joined us. I remember her enormous bosom on which she gathered all of us children, like a mother hen protecting her chicks and praying her Ave Maria repeatedly as loud as she could. Her bosom felt like a down-stuffed pillow. The sirens would howl when the raids started and stop - after that, it was still.

April until July 1945 - American Occupation of Thuringia

From the air raid pressure, our big wooden front door would fly open and close with a never-ending "ding ding ding." I tore myself loose from our group and ran upstairs to shut the door. I saw a tank rolling down our narrow street when I looked outside. I noticed a small can lying in the middle of the street. On the tank sitting on top coming towards me was a very dark-skinned man. While looking at me, his warm smile would stay with me forever. I was no longer afraid. I dashed out, grabbed the can, and a second tank came rolling down the street, squeezing and barely fitting between the narrow streets. This little can bore some delicious spread. Being so starved, it was a welcome delicacy, together with our meager ration of bread, for all of us. At that moment, I had a good feeling about our conquerors.

The Spanish lady left us and an Italian forced laborer came to visit my grandmother, who also spoke fluently Italian. He pulled me onto his lap and my grandmother removed me quickly. During the Nazi time, forced laborers from foreign countries were put on farms, in manufacturing plants, and everywhere where labor was short because the German men had to serve at the front. Now these people could go home.

A miserable bunch of ragged German war prisoners marched past our house. I watched through the window from our second floor. However, German soldiers caught under Russian occupation were sent to Siberia, where they rarely returned from, dying of starvation and sicknesses. Concentration camp Buchenwald was freed.

We were lucky under the American occupation. In school, we were given the most wonderful meals, consisting of a thick vegetable/meat soup and oatmeal cooked in milk with raisins. I remember eating out of an empty can in school every noon. I could hardly wait until the next school day began because I was so hungry. We all were so happy the Americans liberated us. We loved them. But they did not even stay 100 days; originally, General Patton had led them to Thuringia.

July 2, 1945 – Arrival of the Russians

Our territory fell under the Russian assignment. Germany, what was left of it, was divided among the Russians, the British, the French, and the Americans - into four zones. The occupied territories by the Reich had been returned to the Czechs, the Polish, and Russia. After the war was lost, the German people in the annexed parts of the Reich suffered a terrible fate. Hundreds of thousands of German-speaking people were expelled, losing their possessions and leaving behind their houses, farms with animals, and friends. They had settled in those parts for centuries. They were placed all over Germany as refugees. And how the Germans hated them after their arrival. When the Russians invaded Prussia, people fled with their carts and horses over the iced Ostsee coast (Baltic Sea), and which would break under them swallowing horses, carts, and people. The ones that made it with their children traveling along the coast were packed onto the overloaded Wilhelm Gustloff warship, taking off with their last German soldiers, only to be torpedoed and sunk by the Russians when over 8,000 people including their children died in the icy Baltic Sea. The Russians assumed it was a warship.

When Germans fled from the Russians in Prussia, they often were separated from their children, who later were called "Wolfs Children." They would wander about confused, sometimes towards Lithuania, or were picked up by Polish and Russian people.

We also learned that the SS (Schutzstaffel) founded 'Lebensborn' (Fount of Life) and encouraged racially valuable women to bear Aryan children to increase Germany's population of blond/blue-eyed children for future wars. Abortions were not accepted and under this program, blond/blue-eyed children often were kidnapped from their families in occupied countries. Women who had more than eight children would receive the Cross of Honor or Gold Mother's Cross (Ehrenkreuz der Mutter).

After the American troops left us, the first impression I got of the Russian soldiers was that they carried a light red star on their yellow uniforms. Russian soldiers would go from house to house to scavenge food. Luckily, my grandmother had hidden our meat cans from the silos behind our piano. The Russians did not have enough food themselves. There were atrocities and rapes reported. The Russians raped my aunt. She would never recover from that trauma and became an alcoholic in later years, which caused her early death. They dismantled German machines in factories and transported everything toward Russia. We had to learn Russian in grade school, and I would copy most of it from one of my girlfriends who didn't seem to mind.

1945/46/47 were gruesome cold winters. We had ration cards, but their allocated amounts were very small, and they considered my grandmother old. That was the time we learned to starve! The Communistic elite and people who favored them had plenty to eat. We called it *"our hunger winter, 1946/47."*

The relative open borders ended on May 26, 1952. The Communist government claimed to keep out spies, diversionists, terrorists, and smugglers by having barbed wires and all sorts of devices to kill or maim. The borders would be enforced dramatically. There were guards (Volkpolizei – Bundesgrenzschutz), with watch towers, boogie bombs, and other threats.

People living in those areas fled; someone even built his own plane and escaped into the West. Villages were brutally divided by new borders, regardless of families and villages being torn apart, one being in the Western Zone, and the other one in the Eastern DDR.

Berlin Blockade 1948/1949 – Die Rosinenbomber – The C-47 Candy Bombers

It became the first big crisis in the so-called 'Cold War' between the Allies and the Russians. Josef Stalin closed down West Berlin, where all roads from the western parts of Germany into the Russian parts of the country were blocked, and no merchandise could reach the western parts of Berlin. Two million people in these western parts were starving and cut off from electricity and power; however, they were offered by the Communist party to purchase goods in the Russian sector of Berlin. Stalin's aim was to overtake ALL of Berlin and thus stifle free trade and democracy. Before this, the Allies had changed the currency from Mark to D-Mark.

"Monument with C-47 Raisin Bomber - 1948 Berlin Blockade by Stalin

The Allies decided they would land at three airports every three minutes, delivering goods, meds, and coal. Millions of people had to be fed and kept warm. In the beginning, people starved, cut down trees and wooden benches to burn, sat with candlelight and petroleum lamps, and huddled together in beds to keep warm. They refused to surrender to the Communists and patiently waited for the Allies, which were the British and the U.S.A., to deliver help. It helped bond former enemies with new friends and made a lasting impression on the population in Berlin. They built a Luftbrücke (an airbridge) for the people of Berlin to keep them from starving and total desolation. Julius D. Clay, General, was a brilliant organizer together with Berlin's Lord Mayor Ernst Reuter. A wonderful man, Gail Halvorsen, decided to throw little parachutes spiked with chocolates, chewing gum, and boxes of raisins for the children over Berlin – thus the expression *"raisin or candy bombers."* The people of Berlin erected a statue at one of their airports, Airport Tempelhof, to honor the brave men who dared to save and bring democracy and freedom to the battered people of Berlin. Reading up on the history of this exciting endeavor is worth the effort. On May 12, 1949, Stalin gave up the blockade for good.

The only movies they offered us in the Russian sector were synchronized into German; for example, the lives of Maxim Gorki, Fyodor Dostoevsky, Alexander Pushkin, and Leo Tolstoy, to name a few. Most of these films were dominated by drunk stepfathers and beatings of the kids.

The Russians brought grandmother German uniforms, which we had to take apart with razor blades. The Russians seemed to need the material. One day, we received a care package from America, from some kind soul who thought of us. I still have that flowered scarf, which I use as my talisman and as good luck when I travel, covering my clothes in my suitcase.

At night, when grandma was sound asleep next to our small living room, I would turn on the radio around 1:00 a.m. and listen to BBC jazz and news. I fell in love with that station.

The stingy aunt, who owned the house we were allowed to live in, would store apples in her only existing bathtub. Therefore, we were forced to use the open bathhouse once a week. Grandma and I would sit opposite each other in very large bathtubs and soak for hours until my skin would come off in crumbs after toweling.

My grandmother had the annoying habit of humming very loud classical melodies when we walked the streets. I detested that. If I told her, she would get louder, so I would leave her side and walk alone. She was a learned piano teacher and was quite stubborn. I had to practice on the piano every day, and in her opinion, should for hours: *"Child, Mozart practiced eight hours a day. You don't practice enough."* Whenever she would leave on her overland tracks trying to hamster food, I would accompany myself on her piano and sing songs, since I believed I had a beautiful soprano. The endless practice of etudes on the piano was quite boring to me.

One time, two of my little girlfriends and I were chosen by our teacher to dance in front of Russian officers. As a reward, we received yummy sandwiches and a bottle of rum, to my grandmother's delight. Families by now had to lock their larders in front of their teenagers and so did my grandmother because food became unbelievably scarce. She would stand in line for hours, come home one day, and tell me, *"Child when I finally reached the end of the line all they had left were fish heads. I refused to take them."* Anyone owning a garden plot (Schrebergarten) was lucky.

My girlfriend and her family lived in a mansion. Russian officers took over their home, and the family was forced to move upstairs under the roof. But in their garden, they held chickens and grew vegetables. They also had a maid, since they were upper class. But my friend told me the women were ordered to clean up the Russian officers' bathrooms. It was pretty disgusting since the Russians were known for their heavy Vodka consumption. But my grandmother and I did not have a plot, nor was there a garden close to the house. So, we continued to go hungry. We also had some very cold winters and had to dress very warmly.

Since there were no shoes or dresses to purchase, my grandmother exchanged black-market shoes for me, which were not the best for my feet. She took her old dresses and turned them into little wonders. The mothers of my friends admired my red/dark-blue/black dresses, sewn by my grandmother because she had taken sewing classes. I still hear the sound of her old sewing machine in my ears, working with one foot and the clacking of the needle. One thing I did not like was that she made me wear long, scratchy socks, which were very uncomfortable in warm weather. So, I rolled them down to my ankles into a bulge, which looked rather ridiculous. I had a mind of my own and at times I must have been a difficult child to raise. I also missed Dad and suffered from the loss of having a decent home life with younger kids.

Grandma had a habit of airing out her dresses outside after winter chills were gone to remove the smell of the mothballs, which never could be quite accomplished, even after the clothes hung outside for days in fresh air. After having washed their beddings, the women who had lawns would lay out their white sheets on the snow to bleach them out. I have seen that quite often in the country.

During these days of starving and icy weather, we still would ice skate on a nearby lake, my grandmother gracefully skating the figure eight, in her long skirt, looking beautiful and very elegant. Grandma was a very beautiful woman when she was young, with her gorgeous blue eyes, thick hair on top of her head, clear features, and slender body. I can understand why Grandpa fell in love with her. She had a good Prussian character and was very smart and educated. She raised both her boys practically by herself after Grandpa died so young. Dad would tell me she had many suitors, but she decided not to marry again because of her pension. In Germany, widows lose their pensions after remarriage. She also entertained plenty of her boys' friends, who were hungry students, and always had enough food to feed them.

It made me sad when my uncle found a small apartment in Altenburg and moved his family out of the home where I stayed with my grandmother. I liked my aunt and my uncle a lot. One day, I stopped by their place. She was cooking a pudding soup for her family with only water because there was no milk to be had. I smelled that heavenly concoction, but to my sorrow, she told me, *"Child, you must go home. I barely have enough for my family."* The starvation got worse. Elderly people who were unable to work were rationed meagerly.

A day came when we were ordered to a school meeting and I played hooky. With another girlfriend, we met two little boys, at the famous Skat Fountain (German card game) which Altenburg is famous for.

We were spotted and denounced. Word traveled back to my grandmother. She was very upset and scolded me, *"Child, you will end up like your mother."* At that time, I had no idea what she meant.

One night, we were walking past a church when my grandmother discovered mushrooms. Since she was an expert in mushrooms, we picked them and had a fantastic meal that evening. Mushrooms can only be cut at the stem, otherwise, they do not come back. I learned from her to distinguish between the various mushrooms and I am grateful for that knowledge. One Russian word that sticks in my mind is Dasvidaniya (until we meet again).

An uncle, who also lived in our house, was over ninety years old. The story was told that when the only swimming pool we had in town opened early in the year, he would walk a long way to swim. He was in very good shape. Ninety years of age was for us, Methuselah.

By the time I was thirteen years old, my grandmother decided she would send me over the border illegally. I would not grow and we both got thinner and thinner. My three cousins had protruded stomachs, which are typical for malnourished children. My grandmother arranged to have a guide bring us both across the border. We set out with backpacks, mine so large and heavy that I could hardly walk. We were transported in cattle cars. We felt like the Jewish people, who would be crammed into cattle trains, and there were no toilets. Of course, I had to use the toilet, and my grandmother had one of the men slide open the heavy wooden door and she held me in a sitting position. Off flew my pee in the opposite direction. When we arrived at the railroad station somewhere in Thuringia, our guide led us through the woods; the birds chirped, otherwise, it was very still. All at once, because of the heavy burden on my shoulders, I stumbled over a wire, which led in both directions. The guide whispered, *"Start running because the girl hit a radio wire!"* We ran as fast as our legs could carry us. It was quite scary.

Suddenly, we were in the West, and we reached Dad and my stepmother by train, at their little place in Deckbergen, near Rinteln a.d. Weser, where they were refugees themselves. But the reunion was not a happy one. What to do with a child with no extra room? So, they put me up in the only Inn (Gasthaus) in the village, where I had to listen to the noise of drunken men down below. I was upstairs in a cold room with empty beer bottles on the floor stacked in one corner. Since the toilette was down the hall, I peed into one of the bottles. I felt scared, lonely, and totally lost. Then one day, they decided they could not keep me and they returned me to my grandmother. I don't remember the details.

Back in Thuringia

When I returned to Altenburg, times had gotten worse. The food shortage was so imminent that we ended up eating leaves, meant for cattle, cooked with ground-up grains. We did not have the essentials like potatoes, bread, eggs, milk, fruits, and veggies. Vitamins were unknown to us. We ate this mixture day in and day out. Before leaving Warsaw, my stepmother Uschi had salvaged foods, like melted butter, and Schinken (salted and dried ham). We learned that maggots attacked her hams and the melted butter turned rancid while we were starving.

Every opportunity we had was to gather leftover grains or potatoes after harvesting, which would be a welcome change in our diets. Once, when we went *"overland"* I pulled up a Kohlrabi and half the village chased us out of the village, shouting: *"Thieves."*

Before I left Altenburg, my grandmother and my friends behind, my grandmother would tell me, *"Your stepmother will not wash your clothes. You will have to learn to take care of yourself."* She showed me how to separate the pieces. The clothes were scrubbed on a washboard, and the whites boiled in a pot, then rinsed and hung up. How wise she was!

In 1948, at the age of fourteen, my uncle decided to take his family and me out of the Thuringia area. The famine was widespread. Only communistic pals and workers were endowed with food stamps worthy of filling their stomachs. My Uncle Franz came up with a plan to evacuate us, together with another lady, who later drew great pictures of our escape, leaving behind dreariness and hunger periods in our lives. My family and I took a train to the border somewhere in Thuringia. I only know that we were a family consisting of my Uncle Franz, my Aunt Erika, my three Cousins, Nicky, Thomas, and our little Michael, together with this unknown lady who carried a huge backpack on her back.

Again, we traveled on a crowded freight train, which was quite uncomfortable and made me think about what our Jewish families had to endure while being transported to concentration camps. The thoughts never left my mind throughout my entire lifetime. When we finally arrived, we had to cross over open-spaced railroad rails to reach the Western sector, which formed a bridge across one of the Autobahnen (highways) and looked rather menacing to us. It was an adventure, even though scary, and passing from the Eastern part into the Western part – eternal freedom!

We very carefully took one step after the other, from beam to beam, trying to ignore the open spaces in between. Our poor lady companion was not that lucky. Because of the heavy baggage on her back, she lost her balance and landed between one of the open railroad joists, hanging, barely being held by her backpack, which saved her life from falling many feet onto the freeway to her death. To add to the dilemma, my youngest cousin started to scream. My poor uncle tried his best to quiet him.

In the end, he had to cover his mouth with his hand. My uncle's appeasing words to his frightened child did not help. Needless to say, all of us were scared to death the Vopos (people police) would arrest us and take us back to the Eastern prisons, where the adults would never have been released. We, the children, would have been adopted by like-minded citizens of the communist regime. We jeopardized the entire colony of escapees trying to reach the West. This lovely lady made a beautiful drawing of our journey, which I am sorry to say I do not have in my possession. It was a trip that I shall never forget! It was my second attempt to reach the West! There would be many *'Wests'* in my life to cross.

We made it and arrived once more in Deckbergen, close to Rinteln a.d. Weser, where Dad and his wife now lived as refugees, by now in two rooms. My Uncle found a little apartment for his brood, and I once more was at the mercy of my parents, who did not know what to do with me or where to place me. Two times, I ended up somewhere, and in the end on the Bieber's farm. They had acquired a small farm after they lost their large estate in Prussia.

Mr. Bieber was interested in racehorses and took us children to one of the races, where one horse severed the tendon in the front of a gorgeous brown stallion in the heat of the close race. The poor injured horse could not walk, and I was told it would be put down. Being very tender-hearted, this upset me immensely. After that incident, I lost interest in horse racing. One evening, they invited their jokey to dinner. He was a young man of short stature. He ate very little, because he told us, *"I have to keep a certain weight and cannot be too heavy as a Jockey."*

The barn swallows nest all over in European stables and farmhouses, which keeps the stables insect-free. The farmers welcome back their swallows every spring, and they are allowed to build their nests inside the stables. It is a constant coming and going of these ambitious and creative little creatures. I certainly love them. Mrs. Bieber was busy teaching young future housewives how to can meats and run a household. But her cooking was not the best. One of her favorite meals was green beans which swam in bacon grease, which I could not stomach.

So, I would gather plenty of available fresh fruits from their surrounding fruit trees - pears, apples, plums, and cherries and retreat to the nearest available tree, heave myself up with my wins, and supply myself with a good book. I enjoyed the quiet, warm summer air, with the occasional chirping of the birds, by sitting on a sturdy tree limb and feasting on my spoils. I escaped the dreariness with solidity and calmness, unusual for a spunky teen.

Later in life, I met the daughter of the house Bieber in Dad's mansion in Cologne, who married a dentist and lived near the Bodensee in the South of Germany. She mentioned how I would cry myself to sleep every night from being homesick for a home life of my own and Dad. I certainly don't remember anything. By then I was happily married to a wonderful young man and lived with him in the United States of America. I had left the past behind.

The house Dad and stepmother lived in as refugees, was owned by people who had a house painter's business. They employed a crew of men. Once a week, their grandmother would peel potatoes all day long and make potato pancakes. They had to feed a lot of mouths. They were very nice people with one grown daughter. I later heard that the daughter got pregnant with twins, but my stepmother found a doctor who performed an abortion. I wondered why they suddenly pampered their daughter with extra portions of stewed veal and rice and why she had to rest in bed. But sex was never discussed in my family. I still believed in the stork, but thanks to my dear aunt who explained to her boys and to me that babies came from the womb of a woman, the stork story ended.

Across the house painter's home was a garden with statues of garden gnomes (Gartenzwerge), a fountain, and other fairytale figurines. It was quite colorful. Next to that house was a farm where I had to get milk whenever I was available. I carried it in a typical tin milk can. One day, I came too close to this pathetic chained-up farm dog, and he bit a chunk out of my upper thigh. I was bitten three times by dogs, but it never deterred me from loving them and wanting one to call my own.

After rain and storm, I would walk along the village streets and gather apples, pears, or plums that had fallen outside the fences. My stepmother welcomed that. I picked beans as well and earned a bit of money. The farm boy across the street loved the decals I had collected in my small, shabby suitcase. One had to moisten the decal and put the picture upside down on paper, then the image appeared on the paper, after removing the top. He traded me walnuts. I became quite the little businesswoman.

Because of food shortages and goods, illegal trading on the black market was common. The black market in those days went rampant. Anything that could be bartered for food or desired items exchanged hands quietly and secretly. The occupying forces tried to stop these undertakings but to no avail. They threatened with jail. Uncle Harry and Dad had access to linseed and flaxseed and began a business in Karlsruhe, which was in the French Zone, in exchange for cigars. Cigars were important on the black market. Dad could trade cigars for food.

Since my stepmother was squeamish about cleaning fish or poultry, a farm lady taught me how to scale fish, remove the inside of the chicken, and be careful not to damage the gallbladder inside, which would have ruined the meat. I learned to heat soap water and boil my white clothes in it. I learned to till the soil. We were assigned a small plot of land where we would grow veggies. It was something that I really enjoyed.

Later I found out that my mother's ancestors had large estates in Prussia and were ranchers. It is in my blood. My grandmother left me two books, which were written by one of my mother's ancestors. He was the renowned Bishop in Königsberg (Kaliningrad), Prussia, who wrote two books about my mother's ancestry, who very often were ranchers. Very helpful! This way I learned why I am so earth-borne and love farms and animals.

Since I was quite malnourished, Dad would take me around to the farmers to ask for anything they could spare for food. It worked every time. By then, I was in high school and biked every morning very early to reach the nearby little town of Rinteln. My greatest joy was the nightingale as it lifted from the field and offered the sweetest songs I ever heard.

I don't remember anything about that school other than being confirmed in my Protestant faith on April 10, 1949, fifteen years old, in the St. Nikolai Cathedral in Rinteln. A beautiful church, right in the middle of the town, located in the spacious marketplace, where farmers would set up their booths once a week *'to hold market.'* That's when I got my first kiss. They had their yearly fair and a very nice-looking young boy approached me and planted a kiss smack on one of my cheeks. Being very shy, I ran and hid behind the church. From what I heard later he kept looking for me.

Whenever I looked in a mirror, my grandmother would scold me, saying, *"Child, you are looking good enough."* So, I developed little self-esteem and confidence in myself, having been handed around all my life and never having received the parental love and affection children crave.

The first night I arrived, now for the second time, after I had crossed the border the first time and slept in the village's only tavern, I was placed in a house with a war widow and her three children in Rinteln. It was a bitterly cold winter. Since she did not have enough coal to heat, she could only fire up her belly stove in the living room. That was when I froze my fingers. When one of her three children peed its sheet every night in bed, she would take the sheet and hang it right by the belly stove, which would smell terrible. We children complained, but what was the use? My second quarters were with a widow and her daughter, who as a refugee in a farmhouse had been given one room with a small kitchen that held a table and chairs. Since toilets were located in the outhouses and were across the farm building, we did not want to get out at night. Most people used chamber pots that they kept inside their nightstands, but in this case, we refugee kids would use the attic as a toilet. The farmer found out and it ended up in a big calamity!

Once a year, after sugar beets were harvested, the farm women would get together in the painter's house and boil sugar beets in large vets, which stood in the white tiled laundry and were heated with wood or coal down below. The cutup beets were cooked to a thick spread and were used for sandwiches. Rübenkraut, or Sugar Beet Syrup, is a delicious spread on bread and very healthy for humans to eat.

Since Dad told everyone that he wished his only daughter would follow in his footsteps and become a lawyer, a friend piped up, *"What for, she will end up behind pots as a housewife."* When harvest time came for cabbage, the women would shred the cabbage and make Sauerkraut. I had to stand with my washed bare feet on top of a very large stone pot, secured with a wooden lid, and stomp on the lid. After that, a big stone was placed upon the pot and the Sauerkraut would ferment in salt layers.

The village assigned us a small plot of land. Uschi and I would garden in it, and I was allowed to plant what I wanted. I always loved flowers. I never liked cities; I loved farms and farming. Above all, I loved animals. They seemed to understand me, and I, them.

One time, we visited Hameln where the Pipe Piper, according to a saga, confiscated all of the children in that medieval little city. The story went that the Pipe Piper rid the city of rats and mice, but the city authorities would not pay him. So, he took revenge. He decided to lure all of the children with his songs on his pipe out of the city, and they disappeared forever. Since there were no presents to be had, my stepmother found a painted wooden plate with the Pipe Piper on it, followed by the children, which to this day is in my possession, by now slightly warped.

Castle of Teutonic Knights in Malbork, east bank of River Noget, Prussia

1948 – A New Beginning

The Reichsmark became invalid, and the DM (German Mark), 10 Mark to 1 DM, would be exchanged. Everybody received the same amount. The banks were overrun with people standing in endless queues. After that exchange, like a miracle, stores filled up with wonderful goods – cheeses, sausages, hams, anything the heart desired – the Cafés had the most scrumptious tortes, and the ladies would eat two to three pieces of these incredibly delicious creations. Everything could be had, just as in the fairy tale "The Land of Plenty" (Schlaraffenland). We girls would walk past a Café and marvel how someday we would also not care about our waistline and consume tons of torts. On May 23, 1949, our wonderful new Chancellor Adenauer, quite up in age, became our new leader. Hot, delicious chestnuts, roasted on a small barbecue stand on hot coal, were being offered. Dad and I were great connoisseurs of these chestnuts. There was a cheese shop downtown, all tiled from bottom to ceiling with snow-white tiles. Their Dutch Gouda cheeses were stacked high outside on a spotless table and my stepmother purchased plenty for pennies. That was one thing she liked to do: feed me well so I would gain weight. Gouda cheese was my favorite, served on that delicious dark bread they bake in Germany, so crispy and fresh, piled up with butter and cheese.

Dad finally had been denazified (meaning his reputation had been washed clean by the authorities and been cleansed of the stigma of being a Nazi). Dad was allowed to practice law in Cologne. Cologne was a very Catholic city, and my stepmother and Dad had difficulty being accepted into high society, which upset my stepmother enormously. However, over the years, they found adequate friends and were joined by relatives. The relatives finally were allowed by the communists to leave Thuringia.

My Uncle Peter, who had a doctorate in mining, became very wealthy. He married my petite Aunt Sabine or Biene, who was a physician. Her sister Ursula insisted he should marry Sabine and divorce her, his wife Ursula. Aunt Sabine was one of my favorite aunts. She was petite like me, pretty, and a medical doctor. She married her childhood sweetheart from the Russian sector, but the marriage broke up, and later, she married her sister's mining doctor husband instead. Since German ladies are taller, my Aunt Biene had to purchase clothing mostly in children's stores. Most of my pathetic dresses were ordered online from a catalog by my stepmother, who dressed very elegantly and had all of her wardrobe sewn by a seamstress. She took great pride in staying slim, and I heard her say one time to her little poodle, *"I don't want you to have puppies because babies make a woman fat!"*

A very well-known picture historian, Dr. Eduard Plietschke, also a far-removed relative, and his wife settled in the suburb of Lindenthal, where Dad would later purchase his mansion. Eduard had been instrumental during the war by helping the Nazis steal artworks from the Jewish population and enabling the Nazis to acquire artworks. The story went that he insisted his wife would abort her four pregnancies because he did not tolerate children. She told me that she preferred boys instead of girls. So, I never visited them again. They were the most unpleasant people I met.

After the war, most of Dad's friends from Prussia settled near Munich in Bavaria, where Uncle Harry and his family built two very large homes. In later years, Uncle Harry had wonderful fun parties on his estate in a park-like setting, containing a fish pond with surrounding trees. Aunt Edith, his devoted wife, prepared heavenly party foods and barbecues. Adjoining their property was a heavily wooded area, in which Uncle Harry and I found big, eatable, gorgeous Porcini mushrooms (Steinpilze), which he promised he would prepare and share with Dad and me. That night, Dad and I saw the famous Swiss/Austrian actor Maximilian Shell on stage in Munich, where he played the role in a very controversial play, which was being boycotted by a group of people outside the theatre. Dad and I did not agree with this group.

We thought the play was excellent, and of course with Maximilian Schell, whose sister was Maria Schell. Both were very well-known film actors from Austria and in the U.S.A. After we left the theatre, we enjoyed a lovely dinner in a nearby restaurant. It is very common in Europe to visit a good restaurant after every performance. When we returned to Uncle Harry's villa, I found that Uncle Harry had eaten all of the mushrooms. I was very disappointed because these Porcini Mushrooms were my favorites.

1951

At the age of seventeen, in Cologne, which is a city located on the river Rhine and where Dad was allowed to open his law practice, we moved into a medium-sized flat, high up in one of the free-standing houses in the Herwarth Strasse. Through the front door, the small entrance hall opened to the left into one large room, used as his law office. Straight off the entrance was a large living/dining room. To the right the kitchen. The bathroom was next to the kitchen. Off the kitchen was the parents' bedroom. Because of the lack of a second bedroom, they enclosed a small area of the kitchen with two wardrobes and put a bed behind it for me with the few books and toys that were left.

One Christmas time, both were invited out and I stayed behind. It is customary to fill a large, fluted, decorated Christmas paper plate with cookies, nuts, scrumptious Christmas breads, marzipan, oranges, and apples. Each person receives one of these "colored plates," or "Bunte Teller" as they are called in German. Dad shared willingly with me, but that Christmas Holiday my stepmother locked both doors to the living room – just out of spitefulness - so I couldn't sneak in and snack off Dad's Bunte Teller.

Dad was offered, accepted, and specialized from 1951 to 1962 as their Attorney and Managing Director for the Association of German Automats in Germany. It was a very lucrative business. Later, they purchased a mansion in the exclusive Villa areas near the Stadtwaldgürtel (a spread-out green belt), 49 Stadtwaldgürtel, in the suburb of Lindenthal/Cologne.

Our Villa in Lindenthal, a suburb of Cologne

Downstairs, on the small street across from our apartment building was a Ma/Pa grocery store, which my stepmother frequented every day purchasing masses of fancy pastries. A judge would visit us every afternoon to play chess with her and enjoy these scrumptious sweets. Leaving the street on the left was the Ring, a broad street with trams and cars. Wherever streets mounted together, they had a roundabout with a platform in its middle, where a traffic policeman would stand and direct the traffic into various streets. On Christmas holidays, parcels with gifts would mount up around the Traffic Policeman. Quite a sweet sight to see.

Dad employed an Assessor, which is an advisor or assistant to a lawyer until he gets his degree in jurisprudence. He was a rather peculiar fellow with very peculiar habits. A confirmed bachelor, he nevertheless befriended himself with me, by one day throwing plum pits from our window upstairs down on passengers. These passengers found our flat and rang the bell. We would not answer. Thankfully, my parents were not home.

One time, a refugee family with their handcart stopped me in front of our front door leading into the apartment house, if I did not know anyone who would take them in. I ran upstairs and asked Dad who told me that there are refugee camps and they should visit one of them. I felt so sorry for them.

I was schooled into the Königin-Luise Private High School (Gymnasium). However, I was demoted by two years, probably because of a lack of proper education prior to entering this school. I had to start at the beginning of the first class and was not placed in the third class. High school starts at the age of ten. Our class teacher, who taught us English and French, would screech *"You chickens"* if she did not like our behavior. She also would reprimand us for not giving up our seats on a tram, whenever she caught us on a tram. We also had to stand up when she entered the classroom and wish her 'Good Morning', which was customary, as a disciplinary gesture.

There were not enough teachers after the war, so they had to hire what was left or what could be brought back from the "moth box", an expression used in German for long-retired personnel. We had quite an assortment, and not always to our advantage. In the Gymnasium, we had to learn everything - not only German literature, but languages like French and English, with Math, Chemistry, Geometry, History, Biology, Music, Religion, and Sport. I later rose early and learned to garden and cook, because I visited an all-girl school. So, by the time I reached the age of eighteen, it meant leaving the school because I would have been twenty if I had finished the eight years, in which in the last two years I also would have learned Latin. We brought our homework home with us every day.

In my free time, when I did not study or was having a lot of homework, I became an ardent Girl Scout, with an oath binding us to eternal commitment. Our motto was: "One good deed a day." Which we faithfully followed by offering our seats to older people on trams or guiding them across the street when necessary. I totally devoted my weekends to this cause, in my Girl Scout uniform, spending time on my English bike, my guitar strapped on my back, with my backpack, leaving town with my Girl Scout girlfriends, camping in the rain in a too-small a pup tent, but no turning back home even under difficult circumstances.

Biking up steep mountains, spending the nights in youth hostels, playing my guitar, and singing with my groups. The Germans have always been known to sing their beautiful folk songs, of which I have several books. Germans sang throughout history, before Hitler's time, during Hitler's time, and afterward. At the age of sixteen, I led a Brownie group of little girls who adored me, and they would later write to me while I was studying in London, England. I also was chosen to be the leader of my Girl Scout group. We camped, cooked over campfires, learned where the directions were from the way a tree grew, were only allowed to use three matches to light a campfire, and were ONLY girls.

We learned the Morse code and how to use the compass. Boys had no place in our midst. We roughed it, loved it, and cherished it. I would climb a mountain like a goat and be given the nickname "Tom." All of us had nicknames. Standing on a mountain, I longed for the vastness of the universe. We would lay on our backs for hours at night watching the stars. So often, we had shooting stars rain down on us and we would form secret wishes, that we were not allowed to share with anyone. We had to do all of that and learn the constellations, as we made it a game to find the Big Dipper, the smaller one, the Wagon, the Evening Star, the Big Bear, the Little one, and so on. We learned the fine arts of "Orientation" and being able to remember where we walked and find our way back. This also happened when we were let loose in the woods, where we had to get back to our destination. It has been helpful to me to this very day. My group, during camping, once won a cooking contest. We served warm potato salad mixed in with fresh cucumber slices and, for dessert, strawberries with fine German Quark, similar to Italian Mascarpone. And all of this cooked out in the open, from scratch, among various groups of Girl Scouts. I was head over heels for this adventure. I feel very sorry for today's groups, who are supervised by adults, never having the thrill of adventure and excitement we had experienced. To me, this was my life: my bike, my guitar, and my girlfriends.

And the time came to graduate from high school. Dad and my stepmother accompanied me to the ball, where dancing was mandatory. So, I had to take dancing classes. Since we were in an all-girl school, I did not have a date. I had a run in one of my stockings, which my stepmother refused to exchange for a new pair (nylon stockings were scarce in those days after the war). I felt very self-conscious and was not asked by one boy to dance. I remember that night as being dreary and dull.

During the after-war days, my grandmother insisted, as an upper-class daughter, that I would have to take tennis lessons. Riding lessons would have been up my alley, but they were refused. I was very good later in life in skiing, which brought me enormous joy. I did not mount a horse until I came to England, cleaning out stables and learning to groom horses, which I loved with all my heart. I was an outdoor girl. I hated the cities and longed for country living, which was the love of my life.

While being on a farm during summer school vacation, I was assigned to look after the chickens and their coop. I had a yellow fluff of a baby goose following me around, into and out of the house. At first, he followed me with his peepsy voice, but he grew fast and his voice changed until he sounded like a grown goose. Every morning we herded the cows to their grazing pastures and back at night to their stalls to be milked. I helped with haying the old-fashioned way by raking the hay, and the adults would throw it onto the horse carriages. We romped in the hay above the farmhouse and played hide and seek. The summers were far too short!

My stays in Prussia, the estate where I spent time, all of this is only a memory now, for all of these estates are lost forever to Polish and Russian people who are now occupying the country we lived in for over 800 years. We always were good neighbors with our Polish neighbors. The vastness of the lands, the moose that often blocked one's way in front of cars, the mysterious darkness framed by enormous forests, and the waters of the Baltic seas with its famous Amber. I shall never forget my beloved Prussia, the land of my ancestors. Where the winds whispered in the trees and where brave religious men settled and cultivated its land to perfection. Now, other nations have restored the beautiful buildings left by our ancestors. But the Russian Army bulldozed all German cemeteries, and I cannot visit the graves of my two grandfathers or my relatives. All gone for good! But no one can take our memories. They stay implanted in our hearts and our minds, together with all of the memories put down in words.

After Dad settled as an attorney in his flat in Herwarth Street, close to the middle of the town of Cologne, they found a very nice lady by the name of Mrs. Schönfelder, who came every day to clean the relatively small flat. She also would cook for us. Since I had to live behind the wardrobes, my space was very limited. I did not have my own house key and never possessed one, even after Dad acquired the mansion in the suburb of Lindenthal in Cologne. Right behind his mansion, it opened into a large forest, with lakes, swans, ducks, facilities to rent boots, and endless miles of a beautiful 'green belt'. The city of Cologne had been terribly bombed and, like most of Germany's large cities, reduced to nothing but rubble and ashes. It used to house thirteen cathedrals and was the seat of the Catholic Archbishop. Now, only three are left, including the beautiful tall Cathedral as a landmark of history, The Dom of Cologne. Right next to it is the Roman Historical Museum. The streets are busy and hectic with elegant stores and boutiques, which can only be walked (Fußgängerzone). There are big areas in the middle of the large city, the river Rhine flows generously by the Cathedral and a Chocolate Museum has been built along the river, where real chocolate flows out of a fountain and real 4711 Perfume in one of the famous 4711 perfume shops located smack in the city. In A.D. 50, it was called Colonia Agrippina by the Romans, after Empress Agri. Therefore, the name Cologne. To this day, there are Roman sites outside Cologne to visit.

When the cities were being rebuilt, the Trümmerfrauen (the rubble women) were the most likely ones to remove the stones into carts and haul them away. Later, after the war, they received a small pension. To this day, they are called the Trümmerfrauen – as a remembrance of their courage and endurance.

One day, I joined my class on a trip to Paris. We slept in a French Lycée, which is a girls' high school in France. We walked all over Paris, visiting as much as we could take in: Moulin Rouge, the Plazas, and even a nightclub, where one of my pretty high school girlfriends was approached by a wealthy older man who wanted to date her. No one ever fussed over me. I would become a late bloomer (Spätzünder). Of course, most of my classmates had gorgeous designer clothes. One had a Leica camera, one of the most exclusive cameras one could possess. They knew all about Dior make-up and creams, while I felt like a country pumpkin with my *'being unknowledgeable'* and my catalog clothes. These women were apt to marry wealthy men and move in the right circles, while I felt like Cinderella. Our student who possessed the Leica had a 70-year-old father who owned a string of grocery stores and had married late in life to start another family. She was one of the nicest and kindest girls in my class. The last day came around, and we were to visit The Louvre. By that time, my feet were swollen and I could not walk, so I had to stay behind and miss my favorite museum.

However, when I recited long poems by Schiller or Goethe in class, everyone listened, and I imagined myself being an actress. I had the ability to change my voice into different octaves and, therefore, create different characters. I also possessed a beautiful soprano, something that, later on in life, would, through an operation, be wiped out completely. I also tried finding a job as a secretary in a chemical plant in the outer regions of Cologne. I wrote some articles and submitted them to the papers in Cologne, describing my journey through England. None was accepted! As soon as I entered the United States, I found work and would continue working most of my life, using my language skills.

Dad decided to send me to England because my French in high school was better than my English. I wanted to be an interpreter. But first, they sent me to the Vorbeck Schule in Gengenbach, Black Forest, which accepted students who studied languages and took their State Examines to become interpreters. We were three girls placed into someone's house. There, I withered away. During the Holidays, I stayed behind and was not invited to come back home. My two roommates would leave. It was a horrible, lonely feeling. My grades were mediocre, and the wonderful and kind lady Director explained to Dad that I had great talent but did not apply myself. Since I wanted to have a career, but failed so miserably, I think as a last straw, my father saw no solution but to send me to England.

Dad and my stepmother enrolled me in a very expensive plan created by a lady in England, who, for a high pay, promised to place children into English families and have them educated, under a plan of the Cambridge College. The plan backfired. They should have put me into a solid boarding school system because this plan was a scam where very uneducated people in the country took in foreign students for an absorbent price. The lady who sponsored this program lived in a very affluent neighborhood in a mansion on large, beautifully groomed grounds. One thing I really loved about this location was the surroundings and the paths one could hike and walk – called the *'heath'*, where masses of the most beautiful rhododendrons bloomed of overwhelming fragrance. They were not only gorgeous but huge and grew in various colors.

My guest givers lived in a small house and accepted another guest, a young French boy, who was about my age. We were fortunate to view the Queen's Coronation on June 2, 1953, on their TV. We had to take the bus into London every day to attend classes for the accepted foreigner program, which Cambridge College sponsored. At the end of the sessions, all of us received a worthy certificate telling us we had passed and how good our grades were.

But after a while, I lost interest in that family and moved to London into a tiny apartment with a gas fireplace, to continue my studies. I met several German girls, one of whom was a Lesbian and who was interested in my German roommate. I was not her type; how lucky! My German roommate was not very ambitious and soon fell in love with an Italian waiter who wanted to marry her. Also, we were having problems receiving the money sent from our parents through the banking system. So, we decided to look for a job. We found jobs as waitresses in a small Greek restaurant near the opera, where I quickly learned to serve customers and take orders. My roommate decided to drop out and depended on me to bring her some rolls and cold cuts. Our money still did not come, but it kept us above water. Her Italian boyfriend wanted to take her back to Germany and get married. He was in his late twenties and she was barely eighteen or nineteen. I never heard from her again. My next roommate was a sweet French girl. Her mom visited one day and surprised us with French cheese and baguette, that long, delicious, scrumptious bread only the French knew how to bake it right. That is where I discovered my love for French foods. Both taught me to break off a piece of baguette and cut a piece of cheese, then take the baguette in one hand and the cheese in the other. This is the French way of eating bread and cheese.

Since we foreign students had very little money, everyone decided to eat only one meal a day in a restaurant chain called ABC, in which they served forty different sorts of salads. To the astonishment of other English customers, we made it our habit to pile as many of these simply delicious salads on our plates, which would create a pyramid. We would walk the streets of London exploring every nook and cranny, and even took a tour on the street of Jack the Ripper, in a very eerie neighborhood and under cloudy skies. London is known for its many rainy days. When the fog spreads throughout the city, one is not able to see one's hand before one's eyes. We walked for miles, and we used the subways as well. Soon, we were experts in knowing London. We had a lesson from a nice police lady, who warned us not to jingle our housekeys in our hands, which meant we were prostitutes. She told us how the authentic prostitutes would defend themselves from being taken into custody by the police by trying to hack at the eyes of the police with their stiletto heels. We watched a number of high-class prostitutes walking in their fur coats in Hyde Park. It was fascinating to watch the row of cars rolling by slowly making contact.

Hyde Park is also very famous for their soapbox oratories. Speakers stand on soap boxes and give endless speeches. There were many other interesting aspects of London. However, we never saw a play. But the first book I purchased in England was an edition of Shakespeare, which adorns my library as one of my precious possessions. During the time I stayed in England, my Brownie group would write to me faithfully. My little girls, how I missed them. Dad had an English friend who looked me up and we saw Citizen Cane with Orson Wells in a movie house - my first English movie and it was so impressive.

During our school break, my French girlfriend and I decided to hitchhike throughout England, which was quite well accepted and permitted in those days. Nowadays, it's forbidden and much too dangerous. Since I was the spunky and daring one of us two, my French girlfriend suggested I sit next to the driver in case *"he got fresh."* Once, I had a small incident where the driver put his hand on my knee, and I slapped it away. Another time, a truck driver drove us up North towards Scotland. He wanted to take a nap and suggested we three would climb into the back of his truck. When we noticed he had other motives, we grabbed our backpacks, jumped off the truck, and ran as far as our feet would carry us. He apparently was too tired to chase us and must have fallen asleep.

We visited many locations besides Edinburgh and Glasgow. We loved the bagpipes and the natives with their funny brogue. We reached the shores of the Isles of Skye and took the ferry, where we admired that gorgeous island with its sheep and the story that both the island's castle and the neighboring castle in ruins were once bitter enemies. When we left the isle, we caught a ride, but only as far as a lake on the right, which the driver explained was not steep to wade through with a youth hostel across. We looked at each other, decided to wade through this shallow lake, and entered the youth hostel. That night, we had the most invigorating discussion ever, with many young people from many different countries. We solved all of the problems of the world. I fell asleep on the floor next to a handsome and tall American by the name of Cohen. The young man explained to me that his name meant "Priest" in Hebrew and had a special meaning in his religion. I fell in love that night, but all was ruined by his tale that his parents were very wealthy and he was promised to another wealthy Jewish girl. So, my dream ended abruptly.

The next day, we left and managed to make our way to Loch Ness, where we admired the overwhelming flora of tall and breathtakingly beautiful rhododendrons everywhere, contrasting to the bare and almost barren country where no animals grazed other than sheep. I loved Scotland and its history. A cleaning lady in one of the places told me how they longed to gain independence from the British, similarly to the Irish. But we have a story about that in the U.S.A. and in Germany, as well as in other parts of the world.

After Scotland, we traveled South, to the seaside Southend-on-Sea and further into beautiful Cornwall, one of my very favorites. Land's End was truly what it promised, with its iconic St. Michael's Mount, which is a tidal island. All of that is magnificent – particularly Cornwall, England. We returned totally exhausted and overwhelmed with tales and adventure.

We finished our year with Cambridge University's special program for foreign students, and it was time to return to my hometown, which I did with a heavy heart. I was not overly enthused looking forward to a homecoming. I caught the last train out of London at the very last minute. They had added an uncomfortable additional train with wooden benches. The train was crowded, and three young American soldiers were crossing from England into Germany. They had finished their time in the U.S. Army and were as tired as I was. My big neighbor kept bobbing his head on my shoulder, and I would nudge him to move back into his former position. All three of them were of tall, sturdy build. My neighbor across, a nice young man wearing glasses, started a conversation with me, which quite honestly did not interest me at all. He finally asked if we could become pen pals, and I reluctantly agreed.

Upon arrival in Cologne, I discovered to my surprise that Dad had settled into a beautiful stone mansion surrounded by a tall stone wall adorned by two gorgeous rod-iron gates. It was a very impressive building. In the backyard was a gate that led to a building housing the garage. The yard was beautifully landscaped and led to a large covered stone terrace with a stone overhang and steps leading up to it. The terrace had a very large entrance with windows on both sides.

Armored rollerblades were let down from the inside at night to keep unwanted visitors out of the mansion. On the front of the house, a beautiful and large rod-iron gate opened up between the stone wall surrounding the entire property to a very large, exquisitely carved double door, which led into a marble foyer, with a guest toilet to the right and wardrobes on the wall. An inside door from the foyer led into an even larger foyer, again with marble flooring and a large chandelier, from which to the left a door led into the kitchen and pantries and from there another door into the cellar. To the right of the large foyer, one entered a double glass door with practical office furniture, which my Dad's trustworthy and wonderful secretary occupied. Inside her room to the left, one entered the elegantly furnished office in which Dad sat. His domain was from top to ceiling furnished with books, together with his round Chippendale table and the three chairs from Warsaw, nestled in one corner close to one of the windows. The paneled wooden flooring was covered with expensive oriental carpeting. The room had several long and narrow windows with pretty curtains. From the left of his room, double sliding glass doors opened into the large living room, which my stepmother furnished expensively, among valuable antique items. The floor of the living room was laid out with oriental carpets. Back to the left of the room was a door that led into the kitchen, and another door led into the foyer. In that very large foyer, a twisted banistered staircase went up to the second floor, where our white Steinway Grand Piano stood in one corner.

Very expensive antiques were placed around. Another foyer on the second floor and to the left were the private quarters for Dad and his wife, which I did not get to see until after she was dead. In their private quarters was a roomy main bedroom where they slept in their Chippendale furniture, with fancy antique bookcases and chairs, showing my set of books bound in leather and given to me by my grandmother about Roman history. Two very large glass doors would lead onto two separate balconies with a swinging chaise lounge and other rod-iron tables and chairs. Both balconies overlooked the exquisite yard in which a gardener did his wonders. A door would lead off the bedroom into a dressing room with built-in wardrobes covering all four walls and from there it led into the elegant bathroom. To the right of their private entry from the foyer on the second floor was another door opening into a large room, which had been furnished to her taste and turned into a lady's private boudoir, exquisitely with antique furniture. That elderly gardener had a son who was a District Attorney, about which my stepmother marveled that something like that was possible, coming up from a lower class and working himself up. Times had changed by then, for the very best, when the old class system finally ceased to exist.

Outside, to the left of the mansion, a smaller rod iron door led past a very old fountain to the servant's and delivery door, which led into another hallway with pantries, and a huge white kitchen tiled from bottom to ceiling with black/white tiles flooring. There was a dumb waiter leading from the kitchen into the second floor and a board that indicated where someone in the house needed kitchen service.

After my departure, this kitchen would be occupied by one girl, who was allowed to quit her kitchen duties by two o'clock in the afternoon, who would inherit my bike, and my stepmother financed her driver's license, which was quite expensive in Germany in those days. At that time, Mrs. Schönfelder, the former maid would still come, but there also was other personnel to keep the entire floors spotless.

In the basement was a large white tiled laundry room, with a mangle to press tablecloths and linens, a modern washing machine, but no dryer. Clothes were hung up. There was a large room in the basement for canned goods. A dark paneled room for parties with beautiful Bavarian trestle tables and chairs with hearts carved into their backs. Bavarian folklore pictures adorned the walls with Bavarian pillows on the chairs. A four-hundred-year-old carved and covered bed had been transformed into a bar and furnished on its back with boards, old antique brass beer humps, and other antiques. It was so cozy, dark, and cool. After my stepmother died, my husband and I would sit and sip Dad's champagne and wines, which he offered us amply. Next to this party cellar, there was a nicely decorated toilet with funny toilet paper. Behind the large basement foyer to the left was a paneled door, which he slid open and then opened an old iron door with a large old-fashioned key, which would lead down worn steps into an enormously large room with racks on the walls, very cool, filled with exquisite wines he would purchase twice a year with friends. They would make a wine tour to visit the famous and most beloved wineries they knew in their surroundings, covering the Rhine wineries and the side river Mosel, which is my favorite wine because of its smooth and light taste. These moments of savoring his delicious wines will always stay with me.

On the second floor of the house was another staircase leading to the third floor, where a bathroom and two bedrooms were located. I, of course, was put into the front bedroom of the third floor, which was extremely noisy from street traffic, also where the tram would rattle by. It was impossible to open both small windows left and right to enjoy some cool air at night. On all of the three floors were large foyers. The other large room on the third floor faced the back of the house, overlooking the garden. The entire house had been turned into an office, with secretaries and another attorney taking over foyers and extra rooms on the second and the third floor. It was customary and still is today for tax reasons that attorneys and doctors use their own houses as a praxis.

My stepmother was busy running the financial end with a C.P.A. who came daily. By now, she owned a medium-sized brown poodle of sweet disposition, which she kept from me. One day, the little poodle girl came down with a deadly illness. My stepmother was beside herself with grief, but the little poodle girl died. Soon after, they purchased a giant poodle by the name of Ari. Ari had very arrogant mannerisms, and I never warmed up to him. Dad, being very clumsy and forgetful, always having his legal cases on his mind after my stepmother's death took Ari for a walk, and he got run over by a car. Dad was very neglectful at times. Both poodles were beauties with brown curly hair.

My stepmother, by now, had found a great dressmaker who would sew her beautiful clothes which clung to her body. She also had the furrier come to the mansion, where she would choose the best furs for one of her next fur coats. Everything had to be the best. The money flowed.

One night, after a party in Dad's mansion, the guests had left and the owners had retired to their quarters. That night thieves went through the neighborhood and broke into several mansions. When someone in the house let down the roller blades, the thieves waited in the yard, after climbing the tall stone wall and putting sticks under the roller blades, so it was easy for them to lift the roller blades from outside and enter the house. They tried to steal the silver but could not break into the cabinets, because of my stepmother's fetish to lock everything. They poured expensive Cognac into the expensive upholstered chairs and must have stayed for some time. None of us heard a sound.

My stepmother liked to reprimand me for the way I behaved when Dad's company and friends came and wanted to see me. I still had to curtsy, and by the time I turned fifteen, Dad reminded me, and I told him, *"Dad, I am too old for that now!"* His friends found that amusing. I always behaved well.

At that time, my grandmother had moved from Thuringia to Cologne, because the situation there had become impossible for her to survive. She lived in a small apartment together with her beloved piano. She would take her walking stick and pursue her talks in the Italian language at the nearby university. A language she would master exceptionally fluently. When she spoke Italian, which is one of the most melodic Romance languages, it flowed in a beautiful sing-song way from her lips, which I loved to listen to.

By now, I was twenty-one years old. A sweet friendship developed between Stanley and me, and he would visit us in Cologne. After I returned from London, I received an invitation to the biggest and most impressive formal dance party in Düsseldorf, Germany, to which a very handsome journalist invited me, whom I met briefly in London. He told me that someday I would turn into an amazing woman and that I had great potential. When he phoned Dad to ask permission to take me to the largest and most famous 'Dance Party for Journalists in Düsseldorf,' Dad declined the invitation. But my friendship with Stanley blossomed. He took me on a short trip to Switzerland where they snubbed us at the restaurant because I did not understand their Swiss slang. He never touched me and simply treated me as his equal friend. After he returned to the States and visited Dad's stately mansion several times, he wrote to me and proposed marriage. When I told Dad I would leave for the States, he said to me, *"Impossible, I won't let you go. NO!"* I finally persuaded him, and plans were made to start my trousseau, which is customary in Germany that the bride is fitted with china, silver, crystal, and clothing.

Arrangements were made, and everything was ordered. The crystal never arrived because Uncle Harry fell into the bar at one of their parties and broke every glass, so mine were used instead. A black suit and a satin wedding dress were ordered at my stepmother's private dressmaker. I remembered the dressmaker had two beautiful black Doberman dogs, which I was not allowed to pet. But there was a hurdle to overcome.

The quota to the States had closed and no more immigration was granted. Because of Dad's good friends, a German Diplomat in a high position with his Jewish wife Aunt Klara, they pulled strings to get me a Visa to enter the United States. I had to promise Aunt Klara that I would look for a suitable husband for her daughter, who had just been divorced from her unfaithful husband and was left behind with two boys. How would I ever be able to fulfill that dream? Later on, her daughter found a suitable pharmacy husband near Frankfurt.

Aunt Klara showed me a photo of her beautiful sister, who was brutally murdered in one of the horrible concentration camps. Aunt Klara's daughter, whom I dearly loved, had been hidden on a farm for three years, the farmers covered her with hay for disguise, which was stored above the barn.

After constant fuss and disagreements, the day arrived for my departure, with my grandmother going between both parties and with broken promises.

I decided to move in with my best girlfriend and her family to remove myself from that constant stress. On my very last day, I had panic attacks and called home to speak to Dad because I had doubts about leaving my home country. My stepmother answered and told me Dad was not at home. She also told me that they were glad I would leave for good, that they did not want me, and that I should go. That was a very bitter ending for me. Now, I really felt I had no home and no love left for any of them. I turned my back on everything and left for good, never to return until later in life, after my stepmother died. When Dad found out the true story about the reasons for my bitterness, he felt terrible and spread the news among our relatives and his friends, who not only confirmed this but told him it was the truth about his second wife.

Fall of 1956

The next day, my grandmother with her two best friends left with me for the airport to board my most important decision-made flight to the United States of America, where I was lovingly received by Stanley and his nice parents. His mom certainly was a warm and adorable human being who very much wanted a daughter and thought she found one in me. My first impression of a bare and dry Southern California was not very favorable. They had a heat wave during Christmas time of one hundred and thirteen degrees in the shade. I was used to fir trees and lots of greens or snow around me. Now, the scenery was barren, plastered with one oil well next to the other - simply ugly.

Their house was small but cozy. I spent my days watching TV to improve my English. My goal had been to become an interpreter in both English and French. Had I known about the Au-Pair program, where one enters into a family to take care of their children and still could study the language, I would have done so. But my stepmother declared, *"You cost us enough money not also to send you to France."* They had, however, planned to send me to a Finishing School in Switzerland, which was customary among affluent families, to give their children that *'final touch.'* But her furs and jewelry were more important to her. After all, she disliked children throughout her life. She was an enormously selfish and egotistical person, none of whom I hoped to ever meet again.

My cousin Anne, who married my youngest cousin of the Ganske family, told me last year in Portugal, that whenever her parents invited my father and my stepmother for dinner,

Anne had to eat her dinner in her room because my stepmother did not tolerate kids at the dinner table. Their parents were in the wholesale trade and were quite wealthy.

So ended my upbringing and my life in Germany. When I entered the U.S. port, they took away my German passport. Also, I never married Stanley. I broke his heart when I returned my engagement ring to him. From what I heard later on, he visited my family twice in Cologne and danced with my stepmother. Quite strange!

I would enter a totally unknown world to me. In the end, all by myself and with many exciting encounters to come, I was introduced to the love of my life - my tall, blue-eyed, broad-shouldered American husband in Portland, Oregon, on the West Coast, with Mount Hood looming over the city and the ocean nearby. A love affair started, which most likely only is to be found in books. But this is another story.

I never again met any of my relatives from the past, only the ones very close to us. It was a dog-eat-dog world during and after World War II, and people just wanted to survive the inferno.

Jeder ist seines Glückes Schmied!

We all are the blacksmiths of our own happiness!

www.ingramcontent.com/pod-product-compliance
Lightning Source LLC
LaVergne TN
LVHW051038070526
838201LV00066B/4856